D0957470

Secrets of Top Selling Agents

Secrets of Top Selling Agents

The Keys To Real Estate Success Revealed

Joe Sesso

ISBN-13: 9781544986159
ISBN-10: 1544986157
Library of Congress Control Number: 2017904844
CreateSpace Independent Publishing Platform
North Charleston, South Carolina

For my parents:
Thank you for always believing in me.

Contents

Foreword

By Chris Smith
Cofounder of Curaytor and Tech Savvy Agent

For decades, the best real estate agents in the world kept their secrets of success to themselves.

Nowadays, thanks to social media and smartphones connecting us at all times along with a rapid societal shift toward increased willingness to "share," it is officially possible to learn from the best and brightest in the real estate industry no matter where you are or how much money you have.

I was honored to be asked to contribute to this book alongside living legends like Gary Keller, Barbara Corcoran, and Dave Liniger. I've been fortunate enough to be named the most influential person in real estate—an industry that people look down on far too often, unjustly. There are countless agents and brokers who care about their businesses, reputations, clients' experiences, and about getting better and better at what they do and how they do it, year in and year out.

In this book, you will learn from the best of the best. But there is more knowledge in the following pages than anyone could ever act on, so as you read each chapter, try to align the advice with your existing business model, revenue goals, technology preferences, and personality strengths. Remember, passion is what powers profit, not passwords.

After reading this book you will know exactly what to do, how to do it, and most importantly, why you even should. But choose wisely. It can be easy to get analysis paralysis after reading a book like this one, with so many takeaways. Thankfully, the people you will learn from are at the top of their game. They are elite-level performers in a trillion-dollar industry. Listen to them, but more importantly, act on their advice.

Don't just read the book; execute the ideas.

Make a list of action items as you read each chapter, and cross them off as you do them.

The more you read, the more you should *do*.

Good luck!

Preface

The idea to write this book came to me when I tried to find material from some of our past *Secrets of Top Selling Agents* webinars to reference for a presentation. I thought, "What if I could put the 'meat and potatoes' from some of my favorite episodes into a book that could be an easy reference point for real estate professionals around the world?" Writing the book was a no-brainer for me once I had the idea. My only other published work, *The Foreclosure Revolution* (2008), was one of the greatest accomplishments of my life, and I knew that once I had the idea to write *Secrets of Top Selling Agents*, there would be no stopping me. Despite long nights and weekends researching the episodes and the books written by our speakers, writing this book was really fun. Once I had the outline of what I wanted to include on the pages, the rest was simply about organizing the great content from the webinars themselves.

There have been so many great episodes of *Secrets of Top Selling Agents*. I wish I could put them all in this book. Unfortunately, I could only fit so much content onto the pages (but stay tuned—there could be a part 2 someday!) My goal for the book was to draw more attention to the *Secrets* webinar series while putting the words of some of the best episodes into one book. One thing you will notice as you read the following pages is how often the people featured in these chapters refer to each other as influencers, mentors, or close friends. It is a very interesting dynamic I discovered through my research.

Whether you are a brand-new real estate agent, a seasoned veteran, or a small-business owner operating a single boutique office, there is no doubt in my mind that you will benefit greatly from the wisdom presented in this book. I wish you the best of luck and much success.

Joe Sesso

Acknowledgments

This book could not have been written without the assistance of many people. First, I have to thank all the wonderful guests we have had on *Secrets of Top Selling Agents*. Without the awesome content you provided, this book would not be possible. Thank you so much for providing such compelling information for our viewers.

Almost as important as our guests are the producers and hosts of *Secrets*: Deb Helleren and Mel McMurrin. Deb Helleren is the driving force behind *Secrets*. Being from Australia, she has the best accent in the business. But don't let the sweet voice fool you; she is also one of the most determined people I've ever met. When she wants a guest to be on the program, she will stop at nothing to get him or her on. Her persistence has made the appearances of Barbara Corcoran, Gary Keller, Dave Liniger, and others possible. Simply put, the show would not be where it is today without her. *Secrets of Top Selling Agents* is her baby, and she has nurtured it every step of the way, from infancy to maturity.

Mel is a musical and production genius and has produced many songs and jingles for Homes.com, including the *Secrets of Top Selling Agents* theme collage. Mel can do it all, from musical production to sound engineering. He is also one of the nicest people I've ever met.

I absolutely love working with Deb and Mel on these shows. Their passion for the program is evident, and it is the main reason it has gained so much popularity among real estate professionals.

I also have to thank Homes.com. They believed in the free webinar concept and have promoted and sponsored Secrets from day one. For a privately held company, this investment has paid off big time. There is literally a worldwide following for the program, and it never would have been possible without the leadership and resources of Homes.com and its parent company, Dominion Enterprises. This includes the leadership team of Dave Mele, Erin Ruane, and Andy Woolley, among others.

Homes.com is composed of a bunch of passionate employees. This is very evident in the marketing department, where Patty McNease and Monica Torresi, among others, do an outstanding job of promoting the *Secrets* webinar series. They are two of the brightest and most creative people I have ever worked with. I have learned so much from them since 2011, when I first started with Homes.com. Thank you, Patty and Monica, as well as the rest of the marketing department, for doing a top-notch job of promoting and growing the viewership of this program.

Writing this book is only half the battle. Getting it to market is the other half. This could not have been done without some very special people. Jason Parker was the project manager and worked tirelessly behind the scenes of putting all of the pieces together. He took ownership of this project from day one and ran with it. He did an absolutely amazing job! I also have to thank Kevin George for the stunning cover layout and design. I also have to thank my personal editors, George Verongos and Rosa Salgado, and my internal editor, Hannah Graham for making the book flow so well. You guys did a great job, and I couldn't have done this without you.

This book would not be possible without the inspiration of my good friend and boss, Mark Mathis. Mark has such incredible vision. He was the one who encouraged me to produce this work. He's always been there for me, and the process of writing this book was no different. He brought me over to Homes.com to be its national speaker and Midwest account executive at a challenging time for me, and the experience has changed my life forever. Thank you, Mark.

I am also indebted to Dave Fricker, Ron Wieder, Lee Catanzaro, Michael Hayes, Rick Sherwood, and everyone else at Homes.com who has shared the passion for success at our wonderful company. Last but not least, I need to thank my friends and family for giving me the inspiration to push forward when the going got tough.

One

Barbara Corcoran

@BarbaraCorcoran

How to Build a Business Using Innovation, Branding, Leadership, and Guts

Long before becoming one of the stars of the hit ABC reality show *Shark Tank*, Barbara Corcoran founded and owned one of the preeminent real estate brokerages in New York City, the Corcoran Group. Her story is one of struggle as well as triumph, and when she appeared on the *Secrets of Top Selling Agents* program in 2012, she told her story about how she was able to go from waiting tables at a diner to the Shark Tank. It's truly an amazing story, primarily because it is not based on a scientific formula or great invention. Barbara Corcoran shows that through applying the principles she describes on her *Secrets* webinar and in her book *Shark Tales*, which were released at about the same time, anyone can be successful.

Getting Barbara Corcoran to do a *Secrets of Top Selling Agents* webinar wasn't easy. *Secrets* producer Deb Helleren was relentless in her pursuit of Corcoran, who was already a household name nationwide due to *Shark Tank's* wild success. Corcoran acknowledged Deb's tenacity during the webinar, which perhaps reminded her of herself. She said that it was Deb's persistence that finally got her to do the program. We were glad she did, because she was able to tell her story to real estate professionals around the world, as well as provide tips on how to build a successful real estate business.

HUMBLE BEGINNINGS

Corcoran grew up in a large family of nine in a small home in northern New Jersey, just across the Hudson River from Manhattan. After enjoying a fun and educational childhood (she provides details of life lessons she learned growing up in her book), Corcoran graduated from college.

She began work as a waitress in New Jersey at the Fort Lee Diner, where her life would soon change forever. One evening, a tall, dark, handsome gentleman sat down at one of her tables. He was charming, intriguing, and very interested in the blond-haired, blue-eyed Corcoran. After a brief courtship, he suggested that they move to New York City for a life of excitement, which she promptly agreed to.

It wasn't long before Corcoran became fascinated with the Manhattan real estate market. Her boyfriend gave her a $1,000 loan to start up a real estate company, and with that, Barbara Corcoran's business career began. Over the next seven years, the Corcoran-Simone Group focused on New York City sales and apartment rentals and grew from one agent (Corcoran) to fourteen agents and a secretary. Things were going well.

One evening, Corcoran's boyfriend came home and said he had something very important to discuss with her. He told Corcoran that he was seeing the office secretary and that they were going to get married. Corcoran was stunned. She realized that this would be much more than a romantic breakup. It would be a business break-up as well, and it wasn't going to be easy. Her boyfriend owned 51 percent of the Corcoran-Simone Group. After skillful negotiation (which Corcoran describes in her book), they agreed to each take seven agents from their company. Being a minority owner, however, meant that Corcoran would have to start an entirely new company. She proudly named it the Corcoran Group and opened her office in the same building as her now ex-boyfriend's company. As they shook hands for the last time, Corcoran's ex-boyfriend told her something she would never forget: "You know, Barb, you'll never succeed without me." These words became Corcoran's greatest motivator.

Now in complete control of her business, Corcoran was able to focus on building a culture of success. In addition to being an incredible salesperson and marketer, Corcoran was a dynamic recruiter and was able to connect with and woo top agents from across the city to work for her. She used some amazing verbiage that would still work today for real estate recruiting. Here's an example of one of her recruiting ads:

ONE EMPTY DESK

> Only one empty desk available for a positive, high-energy person looking to earn large commissions. Exceptional company. No experience necessary.

In addition to recruiting and training, Corcoran was innovative. She wondered aloud how she could get quoted as a real estate expert in the newspaper. She was told that she needed a publicist. After hiring one, she was advised to produce a report on the Manhattan real estate market. She named it *The Corcoran Report*, and it would go on to become the most respected and followed real estate report in New York City. It put the Corcoran Group on the map as one of the leading companies in Manhattan. It also helped the company grow in size, as many agents from other companies flocked to be a part of the hot new company. They wanted to learn from the leader herself.

DONALD TRUMP

Corcoran tells two great stories in *Shark Tales* that she didn't discuss in her *Secrets* webinar. Both offer great business lessons, and both involve her dealings with The Donald himself, Donald Trump.

The first story details her first-ever meeting with Trump. In 1985, Corcoran put together an issue of *The Corcoran Report* that listed the most expensive condominiums sold in New York City. She listed a unit in Trump Tower as the fourth most expensive unit, based on available data. Before going to print with the issue, Corcoran sent a copy to Trump Tower for The Donald's comments and feedback. Trump not only read the report, he also phoned Corcoran to set up a meeting in his office to discuss it. Needless to say, he wasn't happy.

Upon entering the Trump Tower office, The Donald himself told Corcoran that he was not at all happy with having *only* the *fourth* most expensive condo building in New York City. He then went on the offensive, saying she didn't have all the data on the Trump Tower units. He called one of his assistants into his office to bring in recent sales data. After carefully examining the data, Corcoran told Trump that she had already seen those units in his document and included them in her report. Trump Tower was still fourth. Trump then asked another assistant to review the data with a calculator for a second opinion. Again, Trump could muster no better than fourth most expensive. This did not deter The Donald. Now more determined than ever, he summoned yet another assistant to produce more sales data for Corcoran. Trump proudly showed Corcoran that twenty units had just sold at Trump Tower over the past weekend at record prices. Corcoran studied the new figures. Trump looked satisfied until Corcoran said that because the units hadn't closed yet, she could not include them in her current report. Pending closings didn't count. Only listings that had already closed counted. Again, The Donald was denied.

Knowing that he would not give up, Corcoran tried to find a solution that would make everyone happy. After further analysis, she found that the closed Trump units were the most expensive sales on a cost-per-square-foot basis. Although other brokers had not previously used this method to determine such numbers, Corcoran believed that it was not only legitimate, but that it actually made more sense (and today, cost per square foot has become a standard measure). Pleased with the new outcome, Trump actually helped promote *The Corcoran Report*, which then exploded in popularity and became viral (by 1980s standards), being picked up by such outlets as the *Wall Street Journal.* This both helped grow the popularity of *The Corcoran Report* (which would go on to become the Bible of New York Real Estate) and made the Corcoran Group a major player in real estate brokerage. Barbara Corcoran also had a new friend in Donald Trump—for the time being.

The second story takes place in January 1994 at the Plaza Hotel in Manhattan. Trump owned the Plaza, and a couple of hotel investors from Hong Kong were coming to town to meet with him about a possible sale. The Corcoran Group represented both The Donald and the investors, and the payday would be huge if a deal materialized.

As Trump, Corcoran, and two of her agents waited for the investors to arrive, one of the agents asked Corcoran if they had a signed commission agreement. Corcoran thought one was already in place, but was told at the meeting that in fact there was nothing in writing. Corcoran then turned to Trump and said they needed a signed commission agreement immediately. Trump assured the trio that they would be "taken care of." Corcoran wasn't comfortable with this and insisted that one be signed while they waited for the investors. None of the agents had a commission agreement handy, so they created an impromptu one on a paper doily, which Trump promptly signed. A crisis appeared to be averted.

When the investors arrived, Trump explained to them that while the Plaza was indeed the best hotel in New York, he had something even better to offer them. It was a fourteen-acre parcel in Manhattan called Riverside South. It was the largest piece of undeveloped land in Manhattan, and Trump eventually convinced the Hong Kong pair to buy it instead of the Plaza Hotel. The deal closed for $90 million, and the Corcoran Group's commission for the deal would be 4 percent, paid in monthly installments of $55,555 for six years by the Trump Organization. It was a huge victory for all parties, and no one was happier than Barbara Corcoran. There was just one problem: no one could find the paper doily that Trump had signed. It wouldn't be a problem unless Trump challenged the validity of the agreement in court.

When the first payment arrived at Corcoran Group headquarters, Barbara Corcoran and her team sent The Donald a bouquet of flowers to show their appreciation and to help solidify future business together.

On the day the second check arrived, Corcoran received a call from a very angry Donald Trump. He was furious about an unfavorable cover story about himself in *New York Magazine.* What made him even more furious was the fact that the two other Corcoran agents involved in the Riverside South deal were quoted in the article. He was upset that she had let them speak to the magazine about him. She defended her agents, saying that she thought they had actually made him look better in the article. Trump wasn't buying it and hung up the phone. She then sent him an even larger bouquet of flowers than the one she had sent over a month earlier. This time, however, Trump sent them back to her. This was a bad sign for Corcoran. The very next day, she was served a court summons for breach of contract. The Donald was suing the Corcoran Group and refusing to pay the remainder of the commission. The battle was on.

At the trial, Trump's lawyers went on the attack, accusing the Corcoran Group of leaking sensitive information to the press. Corcoran wasn't going to go down easy. She hired a powerful lawyer of her own, who countered that every quote the agents told the press had already been publicly stated at one time or another by The Donald himself. When Corcoran's attorney displayed the magazines in which Trump had previously been quoted, it didn't take long for the judge to make his decision. Corcoran won the case, and Trump was ordered to pay the rest of the $4 million commission. Barbara Corcoran had taken on the biggest, toughest real estate personality in New York—and beaten him at his own game.

After the Trump victory, the Corcoran Group continued to grow. It became one of the largest companies in New York City at a time when the real estate market was booming. By 2001, it was closing more than $2 billion a year in sales and many companies were watching and considering buying it. After turning down several offers, Corcoran finally decided to sell her company to Cendant for $66 million. She was now a multimillionaire many times over. Although she was sad to walk away from doing what she loved, she knew it was time to get out.

After taking some time off, Corcoran began to get the itch to do something again. She was determined to reinvent herself. She used her real estate expertise to score a real estate advice column for the *Daily News*, as well as a business advice column for *Redbook* magazine. This led to a real estate contributing role on *Good Morning America*, which led to a similar role on the *TODAY* show. It was this exposure that helped her catch her biggest television break—as an investor on ABC's *Shark Tank*.

Shark Tank quickly became a massive TV hit. Corcoran and four other millionaire and billionaire investors would listen to entrepreneurs pitch their companies with the hope of landing an investment deal with one or more of the Sharks.

Corcoran soon became a fan favorite because she took deals that at first glance looked questionable but eventually went on to be wildly successful. Her secret? She believed in the people running the companies. She has been a part of some of the most successful deals made on *Shark Tank*, including Buggyheads, Daisy Cakes, Ava the Elephant, and Pork Barrel Barbeque.

Perhaps the most important aspect of her *Shark Tank* endeavors are the lessons she has learned from the show. These lessons can be applied to any business, including and especially real estate. She shared them on her *Secrets* webinar, as well as in her book.

Lesson 1: TV coverage changes everything. Corcoran learned this in her first season on *Shark Tank*, after the show became a smash hit. When she invested in Daisy Cakes, the company had decent sales. Immediately after the episode aired on television, however, Daisy Cakes sold seventy-five thousand cakes in a matter of minutes and crashed the Internet server. The business grew at an incredible pace, and it was all due to TV coverage on *Shark Tank*.

Although REALTORS® can't always be on TV, there are agents who have done a masterful job of self-promotion and owning a niche. When a network is looking to cover a story regarding real estate, who better to ask than a REALTOR®? This could be a golden opportunity for free television exposure, which, like Barbara Corcoran says, can change everything. The key is to have a plan. How are you going to get noticed? Who can you reach out to, and how can you position yourself as an expert in a particular field? What is your niche going to be?

Lesson 2: The best ideas come from personal experiences. You can read all you want about a subject, but nothing beats the knowledge gained from personal experience. Think about a great idea you have had in the past. How did you come up with the idea? What made you think about it? You probably ran into a problem and thought, "There has to be a better way." This happens all the time on *Shark Tank*.

Personal experiences help inventors ask themselves, "How can I solve this problem?" This is what happened with another Corcoran investment, the Ride On, Carry On.

The idea came from a flight attendant who wanted to find a better way to transport luggage and a small child through an airport—normally a very difficult task. By combining a stroller and a roll-aboard suitcase, the Ride On, Carry On was invented. It solved a huge problem for many parents and made a lot of money for the inventors, as well as Corcoran.

Think about your business. What problems have you encountered that indicate room for optimization? It doesn't have to be a product. It could be a process or service. This is how the best agents differentiate themselves from the rest of the pack. They solve problems and streamline their businesses to maximize profitability. You can, too.

Lesson 3: You've got to have a gimmick. Another hugely successful Corcoran *Shark Tank* investment was Pork Barrel Barbeque Sauce. Corcoran bought 50 percent of the business for $50,000 on one condition: that one of the partners dress like a pig at public events. He agreed, and the Pork Barrel mascot (or gimmick) was born. The company has since expanded into its own restaurants and made millions of dollars.

There are many examples of very successful REALTOR® gimmicks. My aunt and uncle have branded themselves as "Spouses Selling Houses" for many years. Another agent called himself the Superman of Real Estate and actually dressed up in a Superman costume for events and marketing pieces. He is very successful. But a gimmick doesn't have to be dressing up in a silly costume—it could be a great tagline. Chaz Walters in Chicago has had his tagline "Hot Property" for many years and has consistently been one of the top REALTORS® in the Chicago area. His entire brand is built around it. What is your gimmick (or tagline) going to be, and how can you parlay it into dollars?

Lesson 4: Fancy talk doesn't work. Never try to talk over your audience with industry jargon. The best way to connect with your clients or audience is to speak with plain, easy-to-understand language. In *Shark Tales*, Corcoran brings up an example of an investment she made on *Shark Tank* to an inventor of a machine for making all-natural-ingredient sodas. When the time came to give the inventor the $50,000 check, a couple of weeks after the episode was recorded, he had hired a new CEO to run the business. The CEO took over the conversation with industry jargon and other fancy words, but Corcoran was not impressed. She didn't click with the new CEO and decided to withdraw her offer. It didn't make sense to her anymore.

Barbara Corcoran didn't become the queen of New York City real estate because she tried to fake it when dealing with the upper crust. She acted like her normal self for her entire career, and people respected her for it. She spoke in plain language and got her point across in a way that connected with people, and it made her a multimillionaire. Even Donald Trump came to respect her style. Be yourself, and you will connect much better with your prospects and clients.

Lesson 5: Annoying people deliver. Although Corcoran was slated to be one of the original Sharks, she was replaced about two weeks before the season was about to begin. The producers wanted Lori Greiner instead. Corcoran was not going to go away quietly, however. She wrote a personal letter to producer Mark Burnett and flew to Los Angeles for the show as if she were still a cast member. Burnett was impressed by the determination, and Corcoran became an original cast member. (Lori joined the cast in season 2.)

Getting Barbara Corcoran to be a guest on *Secrets of Top Selling Agents* wasn't easy. In addition to being a millionaire, she was a television star with many commitments. But producer Deb Helleren was relentless. Corcoran pointed this out during the webinar and said there was no way she could refuse after personally witnessing Deb's determination. Corcoran respected Deb's determination because it reminded her of herself. Persistence pays, and Barbara Corcoran is living proof.

Lesson 6: Trust your gut. Corcoran said on her *Secrets* webinar episode that there is tremendous power in going with something that just "feels right." She's lived her entire life this way, from her decision to move to Manhattan, to her real estate career, to her deals on *Shark Tank*. Kevin "Mr. Wonderful" O'Leary loves to poke fun at some of Corcoran's investment decisions, but the numbers don't lie: most of her deals have paid off, and some in a huge way.

Ava the Elephant was only a prototype when Corcoran bought 51 percent of the company from founder Tiffany Krumins in season 1 of the show. The kid-friendly medicine dispenser had zero sales and wasn't even in production yet. O'Leary thought that Corcoran paid an outrageous price ($50,000) for such a "silly business." What Mr. Wonderful didn't realize was that Krumins was a savvy entrepreneur who had seen firsthand the power of the product with kids. Corcoran believed in her, and within a few years Ava the Elephant had generated more than $1 million in sales. Corcoran has had many more of these deals on the show, all because she trusted her gut and believed in the people as well as the product.

Real estate is a relationship business. Trusting one's gut is that intangible variable that often separates top producers from average agents. Sure, data and technology play a vital role in marketing, pricing strategy, and sales, but if there's one thing we know about the real estate business, it's that anything can happen. Don't ignore your gut when it tells you to go in one direction or another. It could be the difference maker.

The above lessons were the ones Corcoran discussed on her *Secrets of Top Selling Agents* episode. In *Shark Tales*, however, she continues with her lessons and success principles. The following lessons are directly from her best-selling book.

Lesson 7: You can't fake passion. Let's face it: one thing that most successful entrepreneurs have in common is that they are extremely passionate about their businesses. Corcoran looks for this quality in every investment she makes on *Shark Tank*. The example she uses in her book is a product called Grease Monkey Wipes, which are all-natural citrus degreasing wipes for bicycles and hands. Corcoran initially wasn't interested but decided to explore the possibilities of an investment when Shark Robert Herjavec decided to make an offer. She said she was interested in making a $20,000 investment, but first wanted to hear from the entrepreneurs why she should invest with them. One of the cofounders then stepped forward, looked Corcoran in the eye, and said, "We are very passionate about this, and want to create a global empire. I promise if you partner with us, we will not let you down. I promise you, Barbara, we will make this work. I promise." Corcoran was in.

Are you truly passionate about what you do? It's not a crime if you aren't. Some people enjoy selling real estate as a hobby, for example, and there is nothing wrong with that. However, if you are passionate about being a REALTOR®, there is no reason why you can't be in the top 5 percent of all agents in your market. It is your passion that will drive you to make those extra calls, to knock on a few extra doors, to vigorously work FSBOs and expired listings, and to follow up with past clients. It is that degree of dedication that makes the difference between being a top-selling agent and being an average agent. In fact, one thing you will notice about every episode of *Secrets of Top Selling Agents* is that every guest on the show has passion for what he or she does.

Lesson 8: Dress the part. In today's world, perception is reality. How do you want to be perceived? Barbara Corcoran knew there were some things in her business that had to be of the best quality. She copied the Tiffany's typeface when she created her first business card and used gray ink instead of black. She always came to the office and met with clients dressed for success. Even when she was struggling financially in the early years, her clients and prospects never knew about it, and it paid off.

It is very important to take pride in your appearance, whether it is getting your car washed and detailed or wearing a crisp suit to an appointment. Remember this: your clients *are* judging you, whether you like it or not. Would you rather have them think of you as a sharp-looking professional who looks like he or she has been working deals all day or as a struggling REALTOR® who just rolled out of bed to meet them for an appointment? Appearance matters. Don't fool yourself by taking this lesson lightly.

Lesson 9: Do your homework. When Brett Thompson and Heath Hall stepped into the tank to pitch Pork Barrel BBQ Sauce, they were ready for the barrage of questions that would come their way. Working in the political world trained them to expect the unexpected, and they aced the questions the Sharks fired at them. Corcoran invested in their business, and today it is thriving, not only in the sales of great barbeque sauces, but also as a highly successful restaurant. They did their homework, and their efforts have paid off.

In real estate, it is critical to do your homework. I am not just talking about conducting a CMA or listing presentation. Be prepared to answer such questions as "Why should I choose you as my agent over everyone else?" and "Will you lower your commission rate for me?" and "Why don't we start with a higher price and see what happens?" You must be prepared to answer these questions, and to answer them with confidence. I can't believe how many agents give in and lose their confidence when asked these questions. Often, buyers and sellers ask these questions because they feel they have to. If you can confidently give them a solid answer for why you cannot accommodate them, more times than not they will accept it without question. After all, you are the expert! Do your homework so you can be prepared for whatever comes your way.

Lesson 10: Everybody wants what everybody wants. In *Shark Tales*, Corcoran tells a story about a building owner who was looking to sell apartments in Manhattan that he couldn't *give* away. When Corcoran and her team met with the owner, she immediately had a plan for how they were going to sell them. She said they would price every studio at one price, one-bedrooms at another price, and two-bedrooms at yet another price, regardless of floor or view. What she didn't reveal in her marketing was the location of the building, which created a massive buzz around town. She advertised the listings on a first-come, first-served basis, with location to be revealed only shortly before the sale. When she finally did reveal the location, the buzz was even greater than before. What the developers couldn't sell in more than three years sold out in one day, thanks to the Corcoran Group. Why did this happen? Because everybody wanted what everybody else wanted.

This principle is an interesting one, and very accurate. Look at Starbucks. People will wait fifteen minutes for a latte, but will pass countless convenience stores and gas stations that also have coffee because gas station coffee is "not good," or so they heard. The same goes for real estate. How many times have you seen a property languish on the market for months, but then the house next door goes up for sale and is sold immediately with multiple offers? This happens quite often, especially when the home is priced to sell from the beginning and shows well. Yet the people who lost out on their bid won't even take a second look at the home next door that's still for sale. It is a crazy phenomenon, but everybody wants what everybody wants.

Lesson 11: Step apart from the crowd. The Corcoran Group stood apart from its competition in New York City by publishing *The Corcoran Report*, a real estate newsletter that focused on Manhattan real estate prices. They were innovators who were ahead of their time. The Pork Barrel BBQ guys stood apart by publishing their *Pork Barrel Report*, which focuses on the most wasteful spending projects circulating through Congress. It's a gimmick that works, and it helps raise brand awareness.

How do you stand out from your competition? If you can find a way to do so, it can give you the leverage you need to dominate your marketplace. The answers could be in the pages of this book.

Lesson 12: Expand before you're ready. Corcoran grew the Corcoran Group from six to sixty people with multiple offices in the first five years of her business. She wasn't 100 percent ready at the time, but she did it to get a leg up on the competition. It worked, and the Corcoran Group continued to grow its market share of Manhattan real estate. She compares this principle to putting a gun to one's head. The pressure she put on herself forced her to bring her talents to a whole new level. Countless entrepreneurs have scaled their businesses in a similar fashion.

This principle isn't for everybody. Some people don't handle pressure well, and the stress brought on by growing too fast could be detrimental. Think about expanding a business like expanding a family. Are you ever really 100 percent ready to add children to your family? Most people aren't, but they find a way to make it work. This is how entrepreneurs approach growing a business. They may not be 100 percent ready, but they are confident in their abilities to make it work successfully. How are you looking to grow your business in the next three to five years?

Lesson 13: Be willing to flop. If anyone tells you they have never made a business mistake, they are either lying or have never taken a chance on anything. The Corcoran Group succeeded and grew because it took calculated risks. There were things they tried that were DOA, such as VHS property tours, but it was that same willingness to fail that led them to becoming one of the first brokerages to have a website on the Internet. If Barbara Corcoran had never taken a risk in business, she wouldn't be where she is today.

This principle doesn't mean that you gamble your entire business on something. It means that you should not be afraid to invest in a lead-generation product or something that can help grow your business. Maybe it does fail. So what? At least you tried. As long as it doesn't put you out of business, taking a calculated risk is OK. There is a difference between risk and calculated risk. *Risk* is taking a gamble with no research. *Calculated risk* is taking the time to listen to peers, read reviews, and study the product or service before making the investment. Don't be afraid to flop.

Lesson 14: Shoot the dogs early. The Corcoran Group was truly an elite company to work for. Every year, management would fire the lowest-producing agents. Keep in mind that these agents were being paid commission only, not salary. The reason for their firing: Barbara Corcoran felt that if agents weren't producing revenue, they were costing her money. Most brokers today would never think of purging agents the way the Corcoran Group did.

If you are an agent, you also must learn to "shoot the dogs early." This doesn't necessarily mean firing people (although it can if you have paid assistants). It can mean dropping a marketing plan that failed miserably or a lead product that performed poorly. Don't beat a dead horse—it won't respond.

Barbara Corcoran is the real deal. She could have taken her millions from the Corcoran Group and ridden off into the sunset, but that wasn't her style. To this day, she continues to have the same personality she had as a struggling waitress in New Jersey. This is why she is so beloved on *Shark Tank* by both viewers and the entrepreneurs who pitch their products on the show.

Find out more about Corcoran's rise to the top by visiting Amazon.com to purchase her bestselling book, *Shark Tales, How I turned $1,000 into a Billion Dollar Business*. Filled with heartwarming stories and inspiring lessons, *Shark Tales* will give you the motivation you need to create your own real estate empire.

Two

Dave Liniger

@DaveLiniger

The Changing Market and My Next Step
The Amazing Story of the Cofounder of RE/MAX and His Fight to Survive Illness

When Dave and Gail Liniger founded RE/MAX in 1973, they were considered mavericks. Real estate had always been based on a model where the broker of the office would get a fifty-fifty commission split with his or her agents on all sales. Liniger disrupted this model with RE/MAX, which focused on agents paying a monthly "desk fee" to the broker in exchange for uncapped commissions. The model spread like wildfire, and RE/MAX became a massive worldwide success story. For his efforts, Liniger has won numerous awards. In 2010, *Bloomberg Business Week* named him one of the most powerful people in real estate. In 2011, he won the *Inman News* "People's Choice" Most Influential Leader award. He is also a member of the International Franchise Hall of Fame.

Dave Liniger had perhaps the most dramatic story to tell in his *Secrets* webinar in 2013. The RE/MAX cofounder had just survived a staph infection that left him partially paralyzed and near death. His topic of discussion was the changing real estate marketplace, but he soon pivoted to the story that everyone was waiting for—how he survived his near-death experience. He was a guest on our program to discuss this as well as his book, *My Next Step*. The book describes, in great detail, the tragedy that Liniger experienced, as well as how he was able to survive it with a great support team. Deb Helleren worked hard to secure Liniger to speak on the program.

LIVING LIFE TO THE FULLEST

For nearly forty years, Dave Liniger was the fearless leader of RE/MAX. Starting with a single office in 1973, Liniger scaled RE/MAX to become the leading real estate franchise in the world, enjoying every minute of it along the way. In addition to working hard, Liniger played hard. He was an avid hunter and fisherman who loved the outdoors. He owned a real fighter jet and once even tried to fly around the world in a hot-air balloon. He made the most out of every day of his life. In January 2012, he was scheduled to be the keynote speaker at a RE/MAX of Texas event in Galveston. He had no idea that this trip would change his life forever.

Liniger had been experiencing back pain prior to his trip to Texas. He went to the doctor and was advised that surgery would have to be done at some point, but that he could get by in the short-term with prescription painkillers and a steroid shot. Upon landing in Texas, however, his back pain became extreme. He was so convinced that his back would go out on him that he kept his hotel room door unlocked and advised RE/MAX president Margaret Kelly to check on him in the morning to make sure he was OK.

PARALYZED

Dave Liniger awoke about 2:00 a.m. and realized that he couldn't move his feet. He was paralyzed from the waist down. He alerted Kelly, and she called 911. He was rushed to the hospital. The situation was serious. While Liniger was admitted to the hospital for tests, Kelly filled his slot as the keynote speaker at the event. It was exactly what Liniger wanted while he was hospitalized. "The show must go on," he said.

Liniger wanted to get back to Denver as soon as possible to be evaluated and cared for by his own physicians, so once the doctors in Galveston were convinced that his condition had stabilized, they allowed him to fly home. His son picked him up at the airport, but rather than going directly to the hospital, Liniger instructed his son to take him home. The seriousness of the situation had yet to set in with Liniger. He wanted to be able to relax in the comfort of his own home while quietly hoping that his condition would go back to normal. But it didn't. Within forty-eight hours of returning home, the pain became so acute that he couldn't take it anymore. Liniger had no choice but to go to the hospital.

While at the hospital, Liniger thought he was going to have routine back surgery and would be OK within a few months. The doctors were not convinced that his back was the only problem, because they couldn't explain why his body temperature kept rising. After running tests, the doctors discovered a violent staph infection in Liniger's body that had settled along his spine. Surgery to remove it would be risky due to its proximity to his spinal cord. Permanent paralysis was a real possibility. Antibiotics would be administered first in an attempt to avoid surgery.

As the weeks progressed, Liniger's condition grew worse. One day while in the Intensive Care Unit, one of his tubes became clogged with bile and mucous, which quietly began suffocating him. His heart stopped beating—Liniger flatlined. Doctors were immediately summoned, and they were able to resuscitate him. Dave Liniger had dodged a bullet, but he was still in bad shape. During the emergency, doctors had to rip the breathing tube from his throat, which damaged his vocal chords. (He joked about his voice in his *Secrets* webinar, saying that while he sounded like he had been smoking cigars and drinking whiskey all night, it was in fact the result of his near-death experience).

The infection then spread rapidly into Liniger's organs, and his body began to go into shock. Surgery was the only option, but the risk was great. Because of his condition at the time, doctors didn't know if he would survive the procedure. He was unconscious and couldn't make the decision himself, so his family had to do it for him. They knew that without the surgery, there was no chance of survival. As difficult as it was, they knew that the only chance they had to ever see him alive again was through surgery.

Liniger survived the surgeries, but his condition remained touch-and-go for the next few months. He fell into a coma and then slipped in and out of consciousness. Fortunately, his family's strength never waned, and neither did Liniger's. After months of uncertainty, Liniger's health finally made a turn for the better. He had survived. Whether he would ever walk again remained a question, however. In *My Next Step*, Liniger vividly recalls a moment when he wanted to give up and die. He didn't want to have to burden others with caring for him, and he didn't want to live helpless and dependent. He thought about all the speeches he had given over the previous forty years about never giving up. "What a hypocrite I am," he thought. He realized at that moment that he couldn't give up. He had to take his next step toward survival.

RECOVERY

Although he had survived the surgery and the staph infection, Liniger knew he had a long road ahead to a full recovery (or as close to full recovery as possible). Before he could start rehabilitation, he had to endure one more surgery to repair damage caused by bedsores. This caused an additional thirty-five days of bed rest, but it gave him the opportunity to plan his next step—rehab. He thought about a book he had read many times before that had inspired him to accomplish difficult goals: *Think and Grow Rich* by Napoleon Hill. Liniger credited the book as the inspiration that helped him build both his real estate business and RE/MAX brand. He now needed to apply the principles of the book to his recovery. One of his favorite quotes from *Think and Grow Rich* is "Whatever the mind can conceive and believe, it can achieve." Liniger had been in the hospital for several months at this point, and doctors had told him he would never walk again. He was determined to prove them wrong. This was his first step: set an achievable goal.

STEP 1: SET AN ACHIEVABLE GOAL

In his *Secrets* webinar, Liniger discussed the importance of this first step. He said that in real estate, setting achievable goals is critical. An example he uses is a REALTOR® who sells twelve homes in a single year. If the same agent sets a goal of selling one hundred homes the following year, Liniger says that more times than not, the REALTOR® is setting him- or herself up for failure. An achievable goal might be eighteen, a fifty percent increase in production. Setting unachievable goals can lead to burnout and disappointment. In Liniger's health's case, there was a possibility that he could walk again. His spinal cord was not severed, so being able to walk again was achievable. One thing was certain, however: he was going to work harder at his rehab and with more determination than most people would in a similar situation. If he was asked to lift ten pounds, he would lift twenty.

STEP 2: CREATE A STEP-BY-STEP PLAN

Now that he had set his sights on walking out of the hospital, Liniger had to create a plan for doing it. His goal was to be discharged by June 29, 2012. He devised a plan for how he would make it happen. He put a poster board up in his hospital room with the statement "I am going home on June 29." He knew he had to progress every week to achieve this goal. To start, he would learn to sit up on his own. Once he could do that, he could begin rebuilding the muscle in his legs and arms.

In real estate, agents create a plan to achieve their sales goals by first analyzing where their business came from in the previous year: whether it was from referrals, for sale by owners, signs, calls, etc. The agent would then analyze the previous year's expenses to determine which marketing and advertising strategies worked best. This information would be used to plan strategic growth to achieve their goals.

STEP 3: START THE JOURNEY

Liniger had created his plan to reach his goal of walking again. It was now time to put his plan into action. Every time he went to a physical therapy session, his goal was to do more than he had done the previous day. He learned to celebrate the small victories, knowing that each one was another step toward his main objective.

REALTORS® need to do the same thing with their businesses. If an agent has a clear goal in mind and a step-by-step plan to get there, she needs to celebrate the small victories along the way. These celebrations keep you focused on the main objective.

STEP 4: CREATE A MASTERMIND/SUPPORT GROUP

In *Think and Grow Rich*, Napoleon Hill says a mastermind group is critical to a person's success. For Dave Liniger, it was a support group composed of his friends and family that helped with his recovery. They did this by constantly visiting him and encouraging him to keep going. His support group also consisted of the doctors, nurses, and therapists who were there for him every day. Although the doctors and therapists would never say if walking again was possible for Liniger, his family and friends were there for support and to tell him it was.

REALTORS® need to be a part of a mastermind group as well. They need mentors and trusted colleagues who can help them make a breakthrough and get to the next level. "So who is going to help you get there?" Liniger asked in his *Secrets* webinar. He then quoted Jim Rohn to help the audience define and build their mastermind group: "You are the average of the five people you spend the most time with." You need successful and motivated individuals in your mastermind group.

STEP 5: RETHINK AND IMPROVE YOUR PLAN

Given the progress Liniger had been making in rehab, it was apparent by early June that he would not be walking out of the hospital by June 29. In fact, he wouldn't be leaving at all that day. As disappointing as this was, there was some good news. The doctors said that if he stayed in the hospital for three additional weeks, his progress would be much greater. Liniger had hit a speed bump on his road to recovery and had to adjust his goals accordingly.

Liniger turned this small setback into an opportunity. He rethought his plan and reset his walking goal to July 17.

Agents will also hit speed bumps along their journey to achieving their goals. "The important thing to remember," Liniger said, "is that things happen, and one must learn to adapt and then improve to stay on track." You must always be moving forward.

STEP 6: DON'T QUIT UNTIL YOU ACHIEVE YOUR GOAL

As difficult as therapy was, Liniger never quit. Once he was strong enough to stand on his own, he focused on baby steps. He started by using a walker to help him get around, then crutches, then a cane, and finally he was walking without any assistance at all. Once he could walk on his own, he set new goals. How many steps could he take in a single day? Every day he set new goals for himself. Although he didn't walk out of the hospital on July 17, he did go home. At the time of his appearance on *Secrets of Top Selling Agents*, his goal was to walk one thousand steps in a single day by May 2013.

In real estate, just as with Dave Liniger's therapy, agents need to continue to improve every year. Taking courses, viewing webinars, attending conferences, and reading books are great ways for agents to grow their businesses and to learn about the latest technologies and best practices to improve their businesses.

Dave Liniger is not only one of the greatest success stories in the real estate and franchising industries; he is also a true survivor. His appearance on *Secrets of Top Selling Agents* affirmed his comeback. He also used the webinar as a way to inspire agents around the world to use the same principles he followed to improve their own businesses.

To learn more about Liniger's incredible journey, visit Amazon. com and purchase your copy of *My Next Step: An Extraordinary Journey of Healing and Hope*. This remarkable tale will inspire you to find the strength to overcome the personal and business obstacles in your life.

Three

Gary Keller with Jay Papasan

@GaryKeller   @JayPapasan

The ONE Thing The Surprisingly Simple Truth behind Extraordinary Results

Gary Keller is a true pioneer of real estate. In 1983, he founded Keller Williams (KW) Realty in Austin, Texas, and has since grown it into an international powerhouse with more than 150,000 agents around the world. He currently serves as Chairman of the Board and remains the creative force behind KW's growth and innovation. He and Jay Papasan (VP of Publishing at KW) have written and published four books: *The Millionaire Real Estate Agent* (2003), *The Millionaire Real Estate Investor* (2005), *Shift* (2008), and their latest book, *The ONE Thing* (2013). The pair came on the *Secrets of Top Selling Agents* program in August 2013 to discuss *The ONE Thing* and to show REALTORS® how to achieve extraordinary results in their businesses and personal lives.

Getting Keller and Papasan to appear on the program was the work of Deb Helleren. The pair was not new to the show; they had been guests two years earlier. Their first appearance was a massive success, viewed by what was then a record attendance. Their appearance in 2013 was perfect timing, as *The ONE Thing* was just being released mainstream. Their webinar was another smash success, and so was the book, which became a *Wall Street Journal* best seller. But they didn't just come on the webinar to brush over the main points of the book—they dug deep into it, as you will see in this chapter.

YOUR CHOICES

Keller and Papasan set the tone for their *Secrets* webinar by displaying a triangle with the words "Your Choices" in the middle. On each point of the triangle was a phrase. The top point read "All you could know." The lower left point read "All you could have," and the lower right point read "All you could do." Between the points is the reality, according to Keller.

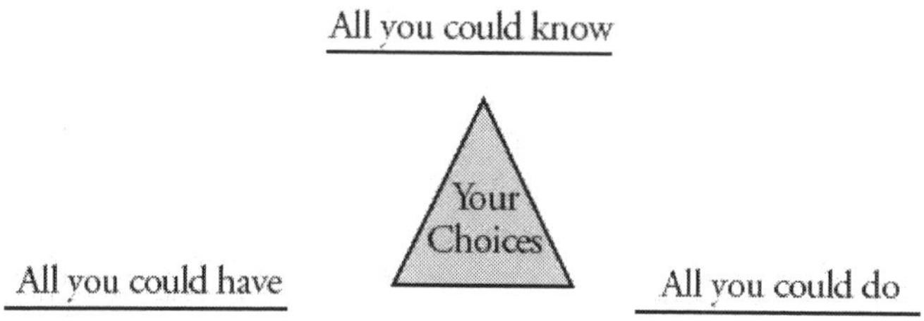

All you could know

All you could have   All you could do

Figure 3.1

According to Keller and the diagram, you can't *do* it all because your free time is too limited. You can't *have* it all because life offers too much. And you can't *know* it all because life is too complex. So how do we make the most of life by knowing, doing, and having what is most important to us? By going small.

GOING SMALL

Everyone has the same number of hours in a day, right? So why are some people more productive than others? They are able to get more done by "going small." They understand that all things don't matter equally, so they find the things that matter most and take care of them first. They narrow their focus to hone in on tasks they *should* do, not tasks they *could* do. By narrowing their focus, they set themselves up for extraordinary results.

THE DOMINO EFFECT

The most successful people take care of the most important tasks first. Doing this creates a domino effect with their other tasks, which is critical in building momentum. Keller and Papasan said that extraordinary success is *sequential*, not simultaneous. Keller discussed his own success as an example of the domino effect at work.

Upon graduating from college, Keller didn't waste any time in his quest for greatness. He sold six houses in the first thirty days after graduation, in a city he had just moved to. He was named Rookie of the Year for his efforts, and by age twenty-six was vice president of the largest real estate company in Austin. By twenty-nine, he owned the largest real estate company in Austin. The next year, Keller Williams had sold more real estate than any other company in Austin. He has maintained his dominance in Austin, being number one in size and transactions for twenty-eight consecutive years. By 2013, Keller Williams was the largest real estate company in the United States, with seventy-eight thousand agents. Do you see how the domino effect can work? Keller says it is not about being extraordinary all day. What matters is doing things that can get you to where you want to go.

THE LIES

Lie 1: Everything matters equally. Let's face it—not all tasks are equal. Keller said that doing just one meaningful task is better than accomplishing one hundred frivolous ones. Often, people put off the most important tasks to focus on knocking out much less meaningful ones first. What usually happens is that people get behind in their tasks and then try to multitask to get more done (another lie that Keller addresses later in this chapter). At the end of the day, the person may have accomplished most of his or her tasks, but the most important task is still incomplete. Achievers, on the other hand, always work with a clear sense of priority. Keller alluded to the "80/20 rule" to drive this point home: the minority of your efforts leads to the majority of your results.

He also illustrated the difference between a to-do list and a success list. By applying the 80/20 rule to your to-do list, it becomes a success list because you focus on the most important tasks first.

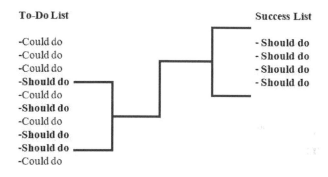

Figure 3.2 (Should-Do List, from *The ONE Thing*)

Above is an example of a "should do" list. Instead of just suggesting what is to be done, it prioritizes what must be done *today*. Identifying the most important tasks helps you work with a clear sense of priority. "But remember," Keller said, "you can have only one priority at any given time." Don't focus on being busy; focus on being productive. "Doing the most important thing is always the most important thing," Keller said.

Lie 2: Multitasking is effective. Have you ever thought about how productive you really are when you multitask? In 2009, a Stanford professor named Clifford Nass conducted a study on how well the so-called multitaskers actually multitasked. What he found was that they were pretty lousy at everything. "How could this be, if these are supposed to be champion multitaskers?" he wondered. "The reality is that multitasking interrupts work flow," Keller said in his *Secrets* webinar. This is why multitasking is a lie. Every time you switch from one task to the next, your mind needs to refocus on the new task. This can end up wasting about one-third of your day. Think about it like this:

The multitasking lie:

Primary work > Switch > Reorient > Distraction > Switch > Reorient > Primary work

Do you see how inefficient this is? Keller and Papasan pointed to four things that multitasking does to short-circuit you:

1. It costs you time.
2. It costs you effectiveness.
3. Loose ends pile up.
4. Productivity will drop.

Don't fall into the multitasking trap. Prioritize your tasks, and focus on one at a time,

Lie 3: You can have a disciplined life. Are the most successful people also the most disciplined people? The answer is yes and no, according to Keller. Yes, they are disciplined in that they have good habits that help them prioritize and accomplish crucial tasks first. But no, they are not disciplined 24/7 in all aspects of life. "Total discipline is a lie," Keller said. The truth is that we don't need much more discipline than we already have. We just need to direct and manage it a little better. The key is to first train yourself to act in a specific way to focus on your important task. You must then turn these actions into habit. "Success is about doing the right thing, not doing everything right," Keller said.

Research shows that it takes sixty-six days of doing the same thing before it becomes a habit, according to Keller. You want your disciplined behavior to become habit. One theory states that it takes only twenty-one days for a habit to form. "It's a lie," Keller said. It's not just about having habits; it's about having the right habits.

Lie 4: Willpower is a lie. Willpower is not what most people think. "It's not just about having the will to say yes to what you need to do," Keller said. "It's also the power to say no to everything else."

Willpower is also renewable energy, which is why it is not always on call. The brain composes one-fiftieth of a person's body mass, but it consumes one-fifth of a person's energy. Willpower has a limited battery life that requires recharging. Keller compared willpower to a cell phone battery. The more you use your phone, the more it drains your battery; likewise, the more tasks you do, the more it drains your willpower.

Keller discussed the Israeli parole system as an example of diminishing willpower. Israeli parole judges are given just two breaks per day from hearing parole cases. A study found that an inmate's probability of being granted parole diminished greatly as the day wore on. That is because the judges grew tired and their willpower "batteries" diminished, making them less inclined to say yes to parole requests. This is why it is so important to do the most important tasks first. As your willpower gets drained, you will be less inclined to get these tasks done.

Lie 5: You can have a balanced life. To achieve extraordinary results, you cannot be balanced, according to Keller. That's because you have to focus your attention on your task at hand, which means taking time away from other facets of your life. Being consistently balanced in work and life is a one-way street to mediocrity. The truth is that greatness is achieved only when the work/life counterbalance ebbs and flows between the two as needed.

Keller said the easiest way to maximize this counterbalance is to organize what needs to be done in a day in order of importance. If there are tasks that are not important, do them later. Having trouble identifying what is important? Think about it like this: What will get you fired if it is not done today? If you do it right away, you will achieve the best results. This requires taking your life out of balance to put all your efforts into accomplishing the task. Pursuing perpetual balance is not the answer to greatness. "The magic doesn't happen in the middle," Keller said. "It happens at the extremes."

Lie 6: Big is bad. "This lie is perhaps the worst of all lies because if you fear big success, you will either avoid it or sabotage your efforts to achieve it," Keller said in *The ONE Thing*. "Thinking big is essential to extraordinary results. Success requires action, and action requires thought."

As your business grows, so does your span of control. How many people can one person successfully oversee? According to Keller, the number ranges from three to seven, but the "sweet spot" is five. Keller discussed his personal example in the *Secrets* webinar, saying that even today, he has only five people reporting to him. Because of this, despite the enormous size of his company, Keller's life is no more complicated than before.

Keller then asked the audience how big their box was. He showed the audience a graph that demonstrated how outcomes are determined by actions. "What you build today will either empower or restrict you tomorrow," Keller said. It's true. Actions determine outcomes. *The ONE Thing* stresses that you have to think big to attain big results.

THE ONE THING

Checklists and to-do lists are popular ways to plan your tasks and make the most of the day ahead. But while writing down tasks is essential, it is not the quantity of tasks completed that is important. Keller discovered *the one thing* when he saw that many people were making long lists of things to do but were pushing off the most important tasks until later. Because of this, the important tasks would often not be completed at day's end. Later, when Keller met with them and asked why the most important task was still not completed, the most common answer was that it was easier to do the smaller tasks first, even though they were insignificant in comparison. This is how Gary Keller came up with his idea for *The ONE Thing*. He encouraged these people to ask themselves one question: "What is *the one thing* I can do, such that by doing it, everything else will be easier or unnecessary?" Keller called this phrase "the focusing question."

What Keller found was that when his students and employees began to ask themselves this question, they not only were able to identify and prioritize their tasks, but also to complete them. The reason? With only one task, there's nothing to hide. After identifying *the one thing* a person can do to make everything else easier, nothing else can be done until the one thing is completed. Questions engage our critical thinking.

"What is *the one thing* I can do?"

"What can I do that will take care of the most important things?"

APPLYING THE *ONE THING* TO ALL ASPECTS OF LIFE

Keller uses his focusing question to achieve amazing results and live a great life. It is so much a part of his life that he also applies it to his health, spiritual life, personal life, key relationships, and finances. Below is a diagram he uses to answer the focusing question for each aspect of his life:

Figure 3.3

Keller used himself as an example for how anyone can apply this diagram to his or her everyday life. He wakes up ten minutes early each day to be spiritual. He said this practice has helped all other aspects of his life. "The biggest mistake people make," Keller said, "is skipping the other aspects of their lives and putting 100 percent of the focus on their job." Doing this will prevent you from accomplishing great results in other areas of your life. Don't let your job define who you are. The following are focusing questions that Keller used as examples in *The ONE Thing*.

For your physical health:
"What's *the one thing* I can do to ensure that I exercise?"

For your personal life:
"What's *the one thing* I can do to improve my skill at…?"

For your job:
"What's *the one thing* I can do to ensure that I hit my goals this week so that by doing so, everything else will be unnecessary?"

Keller reminded the audience that consistency is key. It takes sixty-six days to form a habit, so it is critical to ask your focusing question every single day. Consistency will help you get the answer to your focusing question faster each day and will help you achieve extraordinary results.

TIME BLOCKING
Focusing on and completing your one thing takes time and requires your undivided attention. The reason people do not

accomplish their one thing is because they run out of time due to distractions. They lose focus and are pulled away from their main task by e-mails, phone calls, text messages, etc. Keller said the way to prevent distractions is to time block. Time blocking is making sure that what has to get done gets done. It harnesses your energy and centers it on your most important task.

Time blocking is the practice of allocating a specific amount of time to a certain activity. When you time block, you not only block time off, you also block out distractions.

Keller recommended spending one hour every Sunday planning the week ahead. Block the time you will be taking off during the week, and be sure to time-block your One Thing activities for the week. The key to making this work is to block time as early in your day as possible. Keller recommended blocking four hours per day for your One Thing. You even want to block off your planning time.

PROTECTING YOUR TIME BLOCK

"Time blocking isn't hard," Keller said. "Protecting it, however, is." It is your job to protect your time blocks from all those who don't know what matters most to you. Keller offered four steps for protecting your time block.

1. **Build a bunker**. This is for privacy. Where can you go that takes you out of the path of disruption or interruption? Is it a home office? An office at work? Put a "Do Not Disturb" sign up during your time-blocking hours. This will alert others that you are busy at work and not to be bothered.

2. **Store provisions**. Have food, drink, and your materials stored in your bunker so you won't have to leave to get

them. Other than for a bathroom break, there should be no need to leave your bunker.

3. **Sweep for mines**. Do everything you can to avoid distractions. Turn off your phone, log off your e-mail, and exit your Internet browsers. You cannot be disturbed during this critical period.

4. **Enlist support**. Who is most likely to disturb you during your time block? Employees? Family members? Tell them what you are doing and when you will be available to them. They are likely to be accommodating when you tell them what you are trying to accomplish.

DON'T BREAK THE CHAIN

For your One Thing activities to become habit, you need to practice them for at least sixty-six consecutive days. During this habit-building period, it is very easy to become distracted and break the chain. Don't let this happen. In his *Secrets* webinar, Keller told a story about Jerry Seinfeld.

A newer comedian asked Seinfeld what was the key to building a great routine. Seinfeld said the way to build a great skit was to write one joke per day. Although this doesn't sound like much, writing one funny joke per day is hard work. Many comedians get distracted and break the chain. Keller and Papasan created The ONE Thing mobile app to be downloaded and used to keep you on track toward making your ONE Thing a habit.

THE FOUR THIEVES

Keller said that along the journey to achieving extraordinary results, there will be roadblocks that can slow you down. He calls these roadblocks the "Four Thieves." These "thieves" are the inability to say no, the fear of chaos, poor health habits, and an environment that doesn't support your goals.

1. **The inability to say no.** "One yes must be defended by more than one thousand nos," Keller said on *Secrets of Top Selling Agents*. This means that the way to protect what you said yes to and to stay productive is to say no to anyone or anything that could derail you. He referenced Steve Jobs when he discussed this principle. In 1997, when Jobs began his historic comeback to Apple, they had 350 product SKUs. Being a stickler for quality, Jobs knew that having this many products was unacceptable. Many of the products weren't even produced by Apple! By 1999, Apple had only ten SKUs. This made it possible for them to begin their meteoric rise to greatness. Jobs had to say no many times to get his vision of yes.

2. **The fear of chaos:** Working your time block has negative side effects as well. Untidiness, unrest, disarray and disorder will result when you are laser-focused on accomplishing your ONE Thing. It is inevitable. Clutter will take up residence around you, whether it is with your work, kids or friends. Keller offered frank advice on the subject. "Move past your fear of chaos, learn to deal with it, and trust that your work on your ONE Thing will come through for you."

3. **Poor Health Habits:** "Personal energy mismanagement is a silent thief of productivity," said Keller. High achievement and extraordinary results require lots of energy. The

problem for many people is that they neglect their health in their quest for success. This is a big problem, as it can lead to many health-related issues. Keller recommends a daily energy plan.

a. Meditate and pray for spiritual energy.

b. Eat right, exercise, and sleep sufficiently for physical energy.

c. Hug, kiss, and laugh with loved ones for emotional energy

d. Set goals and plan your calendar for mental energy.

e. Time block your ONE Thing for business energy.

4. **Environment doesn't support your goals:** Your environment must support your goals. Keller stressed that you can only achieve extraordinary results if the people around you support your goals as well. If they are not supportive, they will probably pass some of their negative energy on to you. This can rob you of your ability to accomplish your ONE Thing. The key is to surround yourself with like-minded people who believe in the "positive spiral of success." "No one succeeds alone," said Keller, "and no one fails alone." Pay attention to the people around you.

PUTTING *THE ONE THING* TO WORK

Actions build on actions. Habits build on habits. Success builds on success. When your "one thing" is in line with your purpose and sits on top of your priorities, it will be the most productive thing you can do. "A life worth living might be measured in many ways," Keller said, "but the one that stands above all others is living a life with no regrets." When you look back on your life, your biggest regrets will be the things you didn't do.

Take the next step to discovering your *one thing* by purchasing your copy of *The ONE Thing* online at Amazon.com. For even more great real estate advice on overcoming obstacles and taking your business to the next level, visit KellerInk.com to find all of Keller and Papasan's bestselling real estate titles, as well as great, free resources.

Four

Katie Lance

@KatieLance

I'm #Awful @ Twitter; Please Help

Katie Lance is the social-media queen in the real estate industry. As the CEO of Katie Lance Consulting and the former chief strategist and social-media director for Inman News, Lance has built a huge following of admirers and industry leaders, including companies like RE/MAX. You can hear the passion she has for social media on any webinar or stage she speaks from. She has wowed crowds from coast to coast at the largest real estate events, including Inman Connect, Agent Reboot, Xplode Conference, RE/MAX R4, and many other conferences both big and small. This passion, as well as her wealth of knowledge on all things social, has landed her columns in such publications as the *Huffington Post*, *Medium*, Inman News, and Women 2.0.

I've known Lance since 2012, when I met her at an Agent Reboot Conference sponsored in part by Homes.com. She had just finished a great session on the main stage called, "*I Suck at Twitter, Please Help Me!*" It was such a phenomenal session that I just had to meet her. I introduced myself and was immediately impressed with the excitement and energy she had for her subject material. She lived and breathed social media.

When Deb and Mel invited Lance to be a guest on *Secrets of Top Selling Agents*, the title was changed, but the content and impact it had on the audience was the same. Lance's Twitter webinar rocked the *Secrets* audience, and she has been invited back multiple times to do other social-media talks. (You can find these on www.secretswe-binars.com.) While Twitter is much better known now than it was at the time of Lance's webinar, I'm surprised at how few REALTORS® understand how to use it properly. This chapter is all about Katie Lance's Twitter episode on *Secrets of Top Selling Agents*.

WHAT IS TWITTER?

One of the biggest complaints about Twitter is that people don't understand it or why it is relevant. Lance described it as an "interest network" and the shortest distance between you and your interests. You can search for anything on Twitter and chances are someone has tweeted about it at one time or another. It is a great source for information and knowledge. Lance described some other key characteristics about the network:

- It is live and in real time. (Twitter stories often break before the actual news story does!)
- It is public, and the conversation involves many people.
- It is a way to communicate one-on-one.
- It is mobile; more than 75 percent of Twitter users access it from mobile devices.

Getting started on Twitter is quick and easy. Lance offered a step-by-step guide for how someone can get ramped up in just a few minutes on Twitter. All this can be done using the "Edit Profile" function on Twitter. Here are some tips and shortcuts that Lance offered on how to get set up properly:

A Twitter handle. Lance said to keep it simple, such as @ KatieLance or @JoeSesso. If it is brief and easy to remember, people will not forget it.

User and background photos. These photos need to be similar to the photos you use on other platforms, such as Facebook and Google+. Since you will be using Twitter for business, it will be important to make it consistent with your brand.

A Twitter bio. You have 160 characters to tell the world your story. This includes who you are professionally as well as your areas of expertise. Lance recommended that you also include something personal about yourself to better connect with potential prospects and clients.

WHY TWITTER MATTERS

On *Secrets*, Lance discussed several reasons why Twitter matters in real estate. For one, it is not as personal as Facebook, which makes it more disarming to users. It is also a great way to engage with people and get posts amplified to the masses. Most importantly, the information is genuine. Lance gave a great example of how fast a tweet can go mainstream.

Reggie Nicolay sent a tweet out to his 11,200 followers on Twitter. One of his followers was Michael McClure, who retweeted the post to his 52,000 followers. Then Reggie's wife, Nicole, saw the retweet and proceeded to retweet it to her 11,000 followers. Within seconds, Reggie's tweet became exposed to almost 75,000 people. Now that's viral!

WHAT TO TWEET ABOUT

Lance offered viewers advice about several popular things to tweet about. Popular articles, for one, are great to tweet about, as long as you give credit to the author. (This includes real estate articles.) Photos are also great to tweet about, especially if they are original and fun. An example of a fun picture is to point out a celebrity in a photo, whether by mistake or if you just happen to run into one. You also want to consider posting content about your local community and neighborhood; this content is sure to be read and shared by those who live or work there.

WHO TO FOLLOW

The key to gaining traction on Twitter is to have followers who will be able to see and read your content. By the same token, you want to follow others to learn more about your industry and to gain valuable insight into things you are passionate about. Twitter gives you suggestions on who it thinks you should follow based on your profile and interests. It will also give you suggestions based on whom you currently follow. "Following industry leaders and influencers is always a good idea," Lance said.

TWITTER LINGO

Twitter has its own language and lingo, and it is important to understand the basics. Below are the definitions of basic Twitter terms, as discussed in Lance's *Secrets* episode:

- **The "@" sign:** Twitter handle, use it to tweet to or about something or someone.
- **RT:** Retweet. There are two ways to do this:
  o Click on the retweet button.
  o Quote tweet: Instead of a tweet looking like it came from a third-party source, it looks like you are posting the tweet. This is easier to do on mobile than on desktop, according to Lance. Mobile gives you the option to do either.
- **DM:** Direct Message, or sending a private message to another Twitter user. To send a DM, the other person must be following you.

THE HASHTAG

Perhaps the most misunderstood part of Twitter is the hashtag. The hashtag is a way to search on Twitter for a particular topic or trend. These can be common terms and catchphrases or a trending topic (e.g., #Indy500).

A unique quality of Twitter hashtags is that they are live links. Users can click on a hashtag, and they will be taken to a list of all of the tweets that have incorporated that particular hashtag. Using hashtags is the key to getting your tweets noticed by others. They are also a great way to see what's happening at a particular event or large conference (e.g., #NARAnnual).

Lance laid out some important best practices regarding the use of hashtags and tweets.

- **Tweeting with a hashtag enables your tweets to get more exposure.** Unless your name is Rihanna or Lady Gaga, it will be hard for people to find you on Twitter if you don't use hashtags. People search popular and trending topics with hashtags, so this is the best way for your tweets to be found. Hashtags help categorize tweets and get them more exposure.
- **Don't spam with hashtags.** Make sure that when you use a hashtag, it is relevant to the tweet. Don't overuse hashtags or use popular hashtags that have nothing to do with the subject of your tweet. Use hashtags that are relevant to the topic.
- **Hashtags can go anywhere in a tweet.** It doesn't matter if the hashtag is in the beginning, middle, or end of the tweet. It will get noticed if someone searches that hashtag.
- **Clicking on a hashtagged word in any tweet will take you to all posts that have included the same hashtagged word.** This is a great way to search a popular or trending topic.

- **Hashtagify.me.** You can use this site to see how popular a hashtag is. You also can use it to find other hashtags related to a topic.

BEING #AWFUL AT TWITTER: WHAT *NOT* TO DO

Lance also mentioned a few Twitter taboos in her webinar. These practices are not conducive to Twitter success and are often downright bad. Here is a list of what not to do on Twitter.

1. **Tweeting listings.** You cannot just talk about listings on Twitter. Remember that it is a social network and needs to be more about engagement and less about advertising.
2. **Constantly self-promote.** Don't you hate it when people constantly talk about how great they are? So does everyone else. Don't do it. It will backfire on you.
3. **Post spam.** Don't use Twitter as a spamming platform. People will block you, and it won't help your business.
4. **Create auto messages.** Auto messages on Twitter are so obvious. They don't connect with users, and they won't help you deepen your rapport with them, either. Be genuine and personally respond to people.
5. **Fail to respond to messages.** A direct message from someone is a way to connect and build rapport. It could lead to referrals and more business. Failure to respond to a direct message is not only bad Twitter etiquette; it is also bad business etiquette.
6. **Connect your Facebook account.** There are a couple of reasons why you shouldn't do this, according to Lance. One is that it can be overkill and considered annoying

to post every single tweet on Facebook. Another is that Twitter lingo doesn't translate well on Facebook. The abbreviations and handles don't look good on Facebook. A better solution is to post both a Twitter (abbreviated) version and a Facebook (full) version.

7. **Schedule tweets too far in advance.** Try not to go beyond one week of scheduled tweets. Scheduling too far in advance is not always good, especially when the post is outdated by the time it goes live.

8. **Blindly tweet articles.** Have you ever seen a great head-line that you posted without ever reading the article? Don't do this. You have no idea what the article actually contains. Read it first, then repost it.

Lance not only mentioned the worst Twitter practices, she also discussed several best practices for how to get more followers and how to have a bigger impact on the network.

TWITTER BEST PRACTICES

1. **Twitter lists.** Creating private lists on Twitter is a great way to filter your biggest influencers and prospects into an organized stream. It also cuts through the "noise" of other people you follow on the network. This allows you to view only the posts of people on your list, which is a convenient way to get the information from your most important influencers.

   Lance recommended spending five minutes every day scanning your client list. If you see your clients on

Twitter, she suggested following them and then adding them to one of your private lists (you can click on the "wheel" on Twitter to access the list-creating option). She then recommended reviewing the list daily to see if they have posted any important information or events (such as birthdays, anniversaries, the selling of their home, etc.). This is a great way to monitor your clients' activity and identify buying and selling opportunities.

2. **Create a news list.** This private list is composed of your biggest sources of information. It is not only a great place to get your daily news but also to access the latest information on subjects you care about. You can then retweet and share these articles and posts with your followers. The key is to first follow your favorite news sources and influencers, then add them to the same list. You can also create a few separate lists based on your interests. It is completely up to you.

Creating private lists is a great way to cut through the "noise" on Twitter and makes connecting with people around the world with similar interests easier. You can learn so much about your industry this way. Use lists to build your sphere of influence and better connect with prospects and clients.

3. **Keep tweets short.** Although 140 characters may sound short already, research has shown that tweets containing fewer than 100 characters get up to 20 percent more engagement, according to Lance.

4. **Find local people.** This is a no-brainer. Using Twitter in this manner can help you generate leads, build your

sphere of influence, and farm your network. But how can you find local people on Twitter? Lance said one of the best ways to find local Twitter users is to go to Search. Twitter.com. Using this tool will help you find local users and their posts. You never know when you might find someone nearby discussing an impending move.

5. **Get more followers.** Lance mentioned several techniques that can help you generate a greater following.

   a. **Follow often.** People often follow back.

   b. **Tweet often.** Doing so creates more content and opportunities for people to follow you.

   c. **Be generous.** Give credit to the author in the content you post.

   d. **Pay attention.** If someone mentions you or your company on Twitter, thank him or her. Also look for key opportunities to jump into conversations.

   e. **Be consistent.** Success on Twitter means being consistent on Twitter. Don't be sporadic with your usage. You need to use Twitter multiple times per week to make it work for you.

   f. **#NoTweetLeftBehind.** There are huge opportunities to get more followers on Twitter by simply retweeting and "favoriting" other people's tweets. Look for great content, and engage with it.

   g. **Schedule tweets.** You live a busy lifestyle; the life of a REALTOR® is very unpredictable. You don't always have time to put out great content at the best times of the day. How do you overcome this? By scheduling your tweets to go out at predetermined times. Two companies that Lance recommended were Hootsuite and Sprout Social.

Lance offered some great ideas for maximizing the effectiveness of scheduled tweets.

- Have three to five "go-to" sources to schedule content. You can use your biggest influencer private list to get this info.
- Set up "push" notifications that alert you when you get mentioned or retweeted (the next item explains why).
- Reply to mentions in a timely manner. If you are retweeted or if one of your posts gets favorited, thank the person for doing it.
- Schedule three to five tweets per day to maximize your reach.
- Repeat tweets. There's nothing wrong with this, especially if the tweets are good.

Twitter is becoming more relevant and a bigger part of our lives every day. Lance's *Secrets of Top Selling Agents* episode will be timeless as long as Twitter is around. It is a guide for all types of users, from beginners to those who are more advanced. The techniques she discussed can help one bypass the "noise" on Twitter, find the best content to share, and enable you to connect with influencers and potential clients.

Make your social networks work for you. Hone your social media strategy and learn how to create killer content that converts in Lance's book, *#GetSocialSmart*, available for sale at GetSocialSmartBook.com.

Five

Raj Qsar

@RajQsar

Creating Killer Real Estate Videos

Raj Qsar is a true innovator in real estate. As the founder and president of the Boutique Real Estate Group in Orange County, California, Qsar has been able to successfully carve out his niche in the real estate industry. And the world is taking notice. He has been named to the Inman News "Most Influential

100" list numerous times, and in 2014, he was named as one of Inman's "33 Most Innovative People" in real estate. He's also one of the top one hundred most-followed REALTORS® on Twitter (@RajQsar). He has spoken at such events as Inman Connect, Luxury Connect, Agent Reboot, Xplode Real Estate Conference, CAR Expo, NAR Expo, and AAREA. So why all the buzz? It is for the work that Qsar and his team at the Boutique Real Estate Group have done with the power of video for their company and clients. He shared his top tips on his *Secrets of Top Selling Agents* episode in 2013. The principles and techniques he discussed are still fresh and new today.

I have to thank Erica Campbell Byrum of ForRent.com for helping to get Qsar on *Secrets*. She was an early admirer of his work and introduced herself to him at a real estate conference. She recommended him to Deb Helleren, and the rest, as they say, is history.

Qsar and his company have become so popular for the work they do with real estate videos that people are seeking them out to list their properties. They have created such a loyal following that it is approaching cult-like status, similar to the attention such companies as Uber and Warby Parker have attained. How have they been able to do this? Through a savvy combination of creativity, design, and passion—things they live and breathe every day. These are the same qualities exemplified by Uber and Warby Parker, companies that have been able to take everyday items and activities like taxi rides and eyewear and make them cool. Qsar has established his firm in a similar way.

The Boutique Real Estate Group is now at a point where its team members can do their creative work in-house. They hire home stagers, have in-house graphic designers, and a team of videographers available with the latest and greatest tech toys. They use these assets to focus on superior video tours, backed by a social-media strategy that is second to none in their market.

I visited Qsar and his team in January 2015 at their Corona Del Mar, California, office. Upon entering, I immediately saw what makes the Boutique Real Estate Group so successful: their attention to detail. The office was professionally designed and accented by chic furniture. It had an open floor plan and was blessed by a feng shui master. No detail was missed. Qsar puts the same effort into every video he produces. In fact, on the day I visited the team, they were going through headshots of middle-aged women to cast in a video tour of a property in an over-fifty-five community.

In his *Secrets* webinar, Qsar said that what many REALTORS® think of as video is wrong. "A slide show with music is not a real estate video," said Qsar. "That's the old-fashioned way of doing a property video. Video tours today have to be real videos." He pointed out that despite the technology available to agents today, very few create genuine real estate videos. Virtual tours are not video tours; don't be confused by the two. Slideshows are not videos. Showing the difference to your prospects can determine whether you get the listing or not. Every one of the Boutique Real Estate Group's real estate videos is the real deal.

With demand for real estate videos rising (85% of buyers and seller want to work with an agent who uses video, according to 2013 NAR/Google study, *The Digital House Hunt*), the opportunity to connect with consumers is greater than ever before. "The key to making a great real estate video is to have a great story,"

Qsar said. "Every house and every neighborhood has a story—they just need to be told in a visually effective way." More agents could stand out in their marketplaces if they only invested their marketing dollars in quality real estate videos. Qsar pointed out that many agents don't spend any money on marketing—not even on a quality website for themselves. Quality marketing is not only a good way to sell a property faster; it can also be used as leverage to get more listings. Why would someone hire an agent who is unwilling to spend a dime on marketing? Qsar offered the following tips for creating great real estate videos.

1. **Give every video a story line.** What are the key features of a house? The pool? The yard? The new kitchen? The neighborhood? Take the main selling points of the home and build the story around them. Make sure the video is hyperlocal, meaning that it tells the story of that particular home or town, and make it attractive to people searching in that area or for that type of home.

   Qsar also reminded viewers that it is up to them to create the story. Nobody knows the home or neighborhood like you or your clients. You need to be creative. Don't just make videos about the features of the home. Tell a story about the home, the community, etc. You are the "secret sauce" of a great video. The best real estate videos are the ones that can stir emotions of both your buyer clients and those of potential buyers. If you can connect the story line with the community and lifestyle of the area, your video will be a winner. This is the key to buying with emotion. It's the emotional connection that is made between the buyers and the home that provokes them to make an offer. It can also drive them to overbid for a home if there are multiple offers. When Deb Helleren asked Qsar how he measured return on investment, Raj Qsar coolly said, "When a house sells for seventy-five thousand dollars over the list price, that's a good indicator." Qsar has seen this happen many times and cited a couple of examples, including his company's listing and sale of the first million-dollar-plus property in Brea, California, since the Great Recession. Simply put, Qsar's videos leave a digital footprint that leads to more listings and transactions. They have also been the primary driver in building the Boutique Real Estate Group's brand as the "go-to" company for great property videos.

2. **Have a filmmaker's mind-set**. You don't have to be Steven Spielberg to create a great video, but you don't want to create a *Blair Witch Project*-type video, either. There is a happy medium.

Think about what you would like to see in a video. What features are the main selling points? How can you put more pizzazz into it? What locations, in addition to the home, should be involved? If you live in a historic town or a desirable area, these are huge selling points. If you are going to mention these points in the remarks, they should be featured in the video. They are part of the emotional connection as well.

Patience is a virtue, and never has this been truer than in the making of a video. Qsar says to plan on spending an entire day on the shoot. You want to get it right, after all, and to rush a project that your clients will see is not the way to use video marketing properly. Quality video requires multiple takes, editing, and the right story. Plan on spending an entire day creating your masterpiece.

3. **Add music.** Using music in your videos is essential, but it can be tricky. You can't use popular music that you hear on the radio without potentially being sued or paying a huge royalty because of copyright laws. You also don't want to use low quality music from a virtual tour website. During his *Secrets* webinar, Qsar showed an example of an old video tour with hideous music (it's actually a really funny part of the webinar). So how do you solve this dilemma? Qsar and Mel McMurrin (*Secrets* cofounder) discussed options on the webinar, including sites like Premium Beats, Song Freedom, Beat Suite, and Music Bakery. You have plenty of free or low-cost musical options. This is the legal way to infuse your videos with great music.

4. **Create the higher-end "secret sauce."** Not all houses are created equal. Videos should be treated the same way. You should put higher quality into a million-dollar listing than a $100,000 listing. The commission will obviously be much higher, and your marketing budget should reflect how large your commision will be. If you have a high-end listing, Qsar offers this advice for giving your videos a higher-end feel:

  - **Feature luxury vehicles.** Renting a luxury car for a day to sit in a driveway for a video shoot won't break the bank. At the same time, it helps portray a luxury lifestyle.

- **Include pets.** Who doesn't love a cute dog? Pets stir emotions for many, so consider using one in your videos. If your client's dog is cute and well behaved, use it. If not, rent a trained one for the day.
- **Hire actors.** Qsar doesn't mean hiring Tom Cruise or Christian Bale for your video; just hire a professional actor from a talent agency. Most big cities have them. If yours does, you might be surprised at how inexpensive they are. There is usually no speaking involved for the actors, but you do want to show off glamour and luxury, so having a pretty face to play the part of homeowner or prospective buyer can result in longer views of your video.
- **Take aerial and water shots.** The Boutique Real Estate Group has done helicopter shots, underwater shots, and shots from a boat many times. You should, too, if it is warranted. If your listing is on the water or has a great pool, underwater shots or shots from a boat will help tell the story. If you are selling a sprawling estate, use aerial shots to complement the rest of the video. Yes, you can pay for a helicopter shoot, or just use a drone with a GoPro camera to get that perfect overhead shot.

5. **Find low-cost videographers**. The Boutique Real Estate Group creates a video for every listing it gets. Owning all of its own equipment and having a videographer on staff makes this much easier than it is for the average office. So what can you do to find videographers and the equipment for your video shoot at a good price? Qsar offered great advice:

- **Hire local.** Hiring a local videographer is a great idea, especially if your listing is nearby. The less the videographer has to travel, the easier it is for her or him to get to the assignment. Many will work for less if the job is close to home.
- **Consider wedding videographers.** Wedding videographers are extremely busy on weekends. If they are not filming a wedding, they may be filming an anniversary party, a First Communion, or a baptism. But what are they doing during the middle of the week? Besides editing, not much. They would love to have work during the week, and real estate videos are a much lower-pressure situation than a wedding (you can't reshoot a wedding video). Not only can you hire them for a fraction of what they would charge on a weekend, they also come with their own high-end equipment. Offer a multi-shoot deal and the price may be even less.
- **Shoot a lot of B-roll footage.** If your videographer takes video shots of a community or a neighborhood, you can reuse it for future videos of homes in the same area. This will not only save you money but time as well. Make sure to save your B-roll footage.

6. **Other video ideas**:
   - **Rent video equipment.** Qsar doesn't recommend going out and buying a bunch of expensive equipment right away. It is a huge up-front cost, and you might not like what you buy. Instead, he suggests

renting equipment first. Try it before you buy it, and don't buy it until you've tried it.

- **Download video apps.** Smartphones are not only getting really good at recording video, but editing it as well, thanks to the power of apps. Videolicious is one of the most amazing video recording and editing apps available, and many large brands such as Realogy have signed exclusive contracts with the company to provide this great technology to its agents.

  iMovie is another great app. On a personal note, my beloved dog and best friend of sixteen years, Snorky, passed away in 2015. To honor him, I created a multimedia video of his life, complete with still photos, video clips, and music. I created the entire production on my iPhone, with only iMovie and my Beats by Dre headphones. You can create videos for your listings (lower-end) using this technology as well.

- **Remember that "quality is speed."** Jonathan Antin said this on his show *Blow Out*. The phrase means that we shouldn't sacrifice quality just to have something done faster. The same goes for the real estate video market. Don't rush it for the sake of getting it on the market faster. Quality is worth the wait. Qsar and his team take two to three weeks from the time the listing agreement is signed until it hits the MLS. He actually uses a special seller-exclusive form to be in compliance with MLS rules and regulations, but the payoff is huge because the video is done properly.

Raj Qsar is the undisputed king of real estate video. But he didn't earn this title overnight. He and his team have worked tirelessly over the years to create and produce the best-quality videos in the industry. They have also been able to complement this perfectly with a social-media strategy that is nothing short of genius. Raj Qsar concluded his webinar with some key takeaways:

1. Don't rush the video—"Accuracy is speed."
2. Good videos need a storyline—even property videos.
3. Keep the content hyperlocal—you are selling the neighborhood as much as the home.
4. Post your videos to your YouTube channel and other social channels.
5. Get creative (with stories, negotiations with videographers, etc.).
6. Be original.
7. Have fun.

Learn more about Raj Qsar and the Boutique Real Estate Group online at TheBoutiqueRE.com, were you can also see examples of Qsar's innovative real estate videos, request a consultation, or invite him to speak at your next event.

Six

Chris Smith

@Chris_Smth

Twelve Steps to Increase Your GCI by 50 Percent

Chris Smith isn't a REALTOR®, but he was recently named the most influential person in the real estate industry. To say he has a large following would be an understatement. He cowrote the book *Peoplework*, which raised over $73,000 on Kickstarter and received endorsements from Gary Vaynerchuck and the CEO of

Zappos. As cofounder of Tech Savvy Agent, a real estate tech blog, he began his meteoric rise as a major influencer, gaining more than twenty thousand Facebook fans by 2010. This led him to the national-speaker role at Top Producer and Realtor.com, which led to his chief evangelist role at Inman News. From there he became the chief Peopleworker at Dotloop, which led to his cofounding of Curaytor, a company that focuses on software, systems, and support for salespeople. Within the first six months of its founding, Curaytor was generating revenue in the seven figures—an amazing feat for a niche startup. In addition to running Curaytor, Chris Smith and his cofounder Jimmy Mackin hosted the Watercooler, a web show about real estate marketing and technology.

Smith and I go back to our days working for Move, Inc. in the late 2000s. I was speaking for Realtor.com, and he was speaking for Top Producer. I have personally learned volumes of information from him ever since, and I consider him a true friend and one of the most entertaining speakers in the industry. He tells it like it is, and he's not afraid to use colorful language and expressions to get his point across to audiences around the world. When Deb Helleren asked him to do this *Secrets* webinar, we knew it would be a huge draw, and it was. The principles he laid out are spot on, and if followed correctly, can double one's commission income in just one year.

One thing you will notice in this chapter is the use of case studies. Smith is a master of reinforcing his points with real-life examples, and he discussed several on his *Secrets of Top Selling Agents* episode. He likes to show the "proof in the pudding." As soon as his episode began, Smith got down to business and immediately jumped into his twelve-step program.

STEP 1: INVEST IN DESIGN

"Would you buy from you?" Smith asked the audience. It made perfect sense. If you took an objective look at your website, would you think it was outdated and clunky? First impressions are lasting ones, and your website is one of the strongest first impressions made with consumers. "If people don't trust you, they won't buy from you," Smith said. Good design helps your brand, period.

"Design should start with your website," Smith said on *Secrets*. After all, it's your virtual office, and it is open 24/7/365. It has to look good and perform well. It cannot look outdated and worn out. It also must be mobile-friendly and mobile-responsive. In 2015, Google changed its algorithm to penalize websites that are not responsive to mobile devices, which will kill their search engine optimization (SEO).

In addition to your website, you also must consider design for your presentations, flyers, and even your business cards. Smith discussed some great resources that help agents with design: Haiku Deck (for presentations), Canva ("Design for dummies," Smith said), Pic Monkey (text on photos), 99 Design, and eLance (freelance work at inexpensive prices). It all starts with design.

STEP 2: TAKE THE FOCUS OFF YOURSELF (SOME OF IT)

The old business model for promoting one's business used to be "Look at me; I sell real estate." "The problem is that too many agents focus on ego," Smith said. "They have their headshots on everything, from yard signs to their websites and promotional advertisements to their business cards." According to Smith, that is an outdated way of promotion.

The new way to promote your business is to have fewer photos of yourself and more content in your community, your niche, your logo, and pertinent statistics. This is what the consumer wants to see, not a bunch of pictures of the agent. It's not about the agent; it's about what the agent can do for consumers.

Smith showed an example of Robert Millaway's website as an example of how a top agent's site should look, complete with clean lines, great design, and the focus being on the consumer, not on himself. Smith also shared Millaway's Facebook page as an example of how social pages should look. Again, the focus was on the consumer. Although these designs might look subtle to you, they speak volumes to consumers.

Smith went even further with Facebook marketing by saying that the way for an agent to be consumer-focused in a hyperlocal community was to create a Facebook Group for a town or neighborhood. A Facebook Group is a great way to build a community of people with similar interests (their town or neighborhood), as well as to share information about events and activities. Agents who build active groups on Facebook have much more success with social-media lead conversion than those who don't.

STEP 3: IT'S THE BASICS THAT WIN

Many agents bypass the basics in search of the "secret formula" to make a lot of money. It doesn't exist. Smith said that the agents who perfect the tried and true basics of lead conversion win. Activities like responding to leads quickly, picking up the phone and making calls, doing frequent follow-up, and a having good CRM system are the keys to winning at lead conversion.

Smith uses a great example of an agent who prospects expired listings. The agent prints out the old MLS listing and then critiques the mistakes and verbiage used to promote the listing. This critique offers the seller several reasons why the listing may not have sold. It is a strong approach, and it gets sellers thinking about how they could do things differently when they relist the property. It also gives the agent the inside track on securing the listing.

Smith also said that agents should have every buyer complete a Buyer Intake Sheet. It requires just a few short minutes to fill out, and can reap significant dividends. Why can this form pay off so greatly? Because it helps the agent build profiles for each buyer by asking consistent questions that the agent can enter in his or her CRM database. This makes it much easier to find the best possible property for the buyers based on their answers. It can also make it easier to follow up with buyers. Too many agents neglect to have buyers fill out any sort of intake or information form.

STEP 4: CHANGE THE WAY YOU FOLLOW UP

Traditionally, agents would meet clients or prospects and then follow up with them on a schedule, regardless of interest or activities. Agents with very few clients could probably manage their business this way, but as their client base grows, it becomes much more difficult. Many deals are lost due to infrequent follow-up and agents failing to identify hot leads.

Smith said that the best agents follow up based on client activity. Through the use of a good CRM system, agents today can see when their clients opened an e-mail message, as well as which listings they viewed. Savvy agents jump on this information and follow up with their prospect soon after their action (opening an e-mail, viewing a listing, etc.). By focusing on top-of-mind awareness, agents can convert more leads.

STEP 5: STOP GUESSING ABOUT ROI

Tom Ferry said that the biggest mistake agents make is that they don't know the Return on Investment (ROI) on the products they purchase. Smith agreed that this is a major mistake. Many agents don't know how to measure it correctly, which is why Smith shared the formula on *Secrets of Top Selling Agents*:

1. Step 1: Add up your year-to-date lead total by source.
2. Step 2: Calculate your year-to-date closings from the MLS.
3. Step 3: Add your average revenue per closing, then subtract the cost of the lead.

Smith discussed an example on *Secrets* about an agent who wanted to cancel her Homes.com subscription. He had her enter her data into the formula. The agent had closed six deals from Homes.com leads that year, which accounted for $36,000 in total commissions. Her cost of the leads from Homes.com was $2,400 for the year. Here's the breakdown:

- Six Homes.com deals closed for $36,000—an average commission of $6,000 per deal.
- Cost of leads from Homes.com for the year = $2,400.
- $36,000 – $2,400 = $33,600, her net profit from the Homes.com subscription.

The agent spent $2,400 and reaped a profit of $33,600 in a single year from Homes.com. That came out to a return of fifteen times her investment. Needless to say, she decided not to cancel her Homes.com subscription. "The lesson to be learned is to stop guessing and start tracking," Smith said.

STEP 6: FOLLOW UP WITH PAST CLIENTS VIA E-MAIL

Too many agents think that just because they have access to "drip" marketing campaigns, they should put every single client in one, even if it doesn't make sense. This is a big no-no according to Smith. He said it is not a good practice to "drip" on past clients unnecessarily. There is nothing wrong with putting someone in a "drip" campaign, but it must make sense.

One of the best practices Smith recommended in his episode was to follow up with creative e-mails to your sphere of influence. These are the people who know you best. You must be more creative when messaging them. Smith said that every e-mail you send to past clients and your sphere should do one of three things:

1. Educate (about real estate or other subjects that matter).
2. Entertain (viral videos, how-to, etc.).
3. Create a conversation (challenge them to respond).

STEP 7: GO BIG, AND DON'T AUTOMATE EVERYTHING

Do you want to go the extra mile for your client? Then you need to think differently than the majority of REALTORS®. One of the key places of a transaction where you can be remembered and referred by your clients is at closing. You did a great job handling the transaction, but then again, your clients expected things to go well. A unique closing gift is a great way for your clients to remember you. Smith gave an example of an agent who sent a gift to the hotel where his clients were staying for their vacation. It was waiting for them in their room when they arrived, and they were extremely impressed. A great gift doesn't have to be expensive, just memorable.

One of the best ways to hear about an important event in your clients' lives is through social media. If they are excited about something, they are probably pushing it on one or more of their networks. This is a great opportunity to make their transaction even better. This is how you stand out.

STEP 8: INVEST (LITERALLY) IN CONTENT

Content is king today when it comes to blogging and posting on social channels. Smith said agents basically have two choices for producing good content: invest time in writing quality content for your blog and social channels or pay a company or individual to do it for you. You have to be an influencer, and posting consistent, quality content is the way to be one.

After creating the content (or having someone create it for you), you need to get it in front of people—a lot of them. The best way to do this is with Facebook ads. Boosting your posts is not expensive and can quickly build an audience. "It's a core strategy for growth," Smith said.

STEP 9: SHOWCASE YOUR RESPONSE TIME

Too many agents spend time talking about their accomplishments to buyers and sellers. Although agents may think they are convincing the prospect to work with them, it often backfires because it comes off as narcissistic.

A better approach is to focus on your performance. Showing clients performance indicators such as how you are using technology to optimize response time to buyer leads differentiates you from your competition and uses a performance-based approach to building rapport. Clients want actions, not words. Focus on performance actions.

STEP 10: ADVERTISE ON FACEBOOK

Smith touched on promoting Facebook posts in step 8, but he focuses solely on the practice in this step. He is a big believer in promoting posts, because he has seen many of his REALTOR® clients enjoy massive success from it. He said agents should promote both active listing posts and sold listing posts, and he showed a great example of the Joe Taylor Group in Las Vegas and how they have leveraged this technique to generate much success (you can see these ads on Smith's *Secrets of Top Selling Agents* episode). What makes these promoted posts so effective is the massive amount of data that Facebook has. You can use the data to zero in on a specific demographic, such as a neighborhood, an income level, special interests, or a combination of items. It is this specific ad targeting that can generate lots of leads from Facebook.

Smith said a best practice for your ad is to provide the details of the property, but make visitors click through to get the price. The following step will show you what to do next.

STEP 11: CREATE SIMPLE LANDING PAGES

Simple landing pages are inbound, single-lead capture pages. Curaytor builds its own landing pages for clients, but Smith also mentioned two other companies that agents can use to build these type of landing pages: Unbounce and Lead Pages. When their REALTOR® clients run a Facebook-promoted post campaign, they have two powerful weapons at their disposal: Facebook's data, to focus on a campaign, and a single landing page to capture the leads from the campaign. Smith said the use of single landing pages for Facebook ads has been very successful in maximizing lead generation for agents. The next step shows how these pages can generate a ton of seller leads.

STEP 12: BUILD SELLER LEAD GENERATION

Farming has been a part of real estate since the beginning of the industry. Smith said farming is still very much alive, but mostly in a digital sense. Social-savvy agents are creating community pages on Facebook to attract and encourage members of the community to contribute to the pages. This type of farming is a powerful way to generate seller leads. Connecting with members in your community online can enable you to get home valuation requests and other seller-related questions.

Smith brought up success stories of his clients on his *Secrets* episode. In one year, his client Sarita Dua generated 582 leads using various digital farming strategies. Robert Millaway generated more than 600 in one year. Smith even showed the audience some of the different ads Dua used to generate her windfall of leads (check out the ads on the *Secrets of Top Selling Agents* episode).

KEY TAKEAWAYS

Smith concluded his *Secrets* episode by reminding the audience that before they do anything, they have to have their systems in place. Once this is done, he said to remember the following:

1. Follow up with hot leads immediately.
2. Follow up with old leads optimistically.
3. Call your sphere of influence without fail.
4. Run effective ads to generate leads.
5. Constantly focus on building your brand or image.
6. Have good drip marketing campaigns.

Discover even more ways to increase your commissions by purchasing Chris Smith's latest bestselling book *The Conversion Code*. This guide is packed with the tips you need to capture internet leads, create quality appointments, and close more sales. Visit theConversionCode.com for more information.

Seven

Jay Baer with Erica Campbell Byrum

@JayBaer

@EricaCampbell

Youtility for Real Estate

Jay Baer is a digital marketing expert who has helped more than seven hundred brands achieve digital-marketing and social-media success. Since 1994, he has helped companies such as Nike, Walmart, Allstate, and Best Buy develop and implement digital marketing and social-media strategies to help grow their online reach. He is the president of Convince & Convert, a firm that helps companies large and small accelerate their digital marketing results through content creation and social media. The Content Marketing Institute named his Convince & Convert blog (www. convinceandconvert.com) the number one content-marketing blog in the world. The content is both informative and entertaining.

Getting Jay Baer on *Secrets of Top Selling Agents* was the work of Erica Campbell Byrum, the social-media director at ForRent. com. After watching Baer speak at a conference, Campbell Byrum introduced herself and asked him if he would speak to her team at Homes.com headquarters in Norfolk, Virginia. Baer agreed. Her team was blown away by his presentation on *Youtility*, seeing firsthand how their content could have a bigger impact on consumers. Baer explained to them why the content they created needed to have a consistent interface with the company. As a gift to her team, Campbell Byrum gave each member a copy of *Youtility* so they could immediately practice the principles described in the book in their work. The results quickly became noticeable, the cancellation rate of Homes.com social-media products dropping dramatically.

A few months later, Campbell Byrum commented to Baer how useful the principles of *Youtility* could be to the real estate industry and real estate professionals. Baer agreed, and the idea behind *Youtility for Real Estate* was born. In November 2014, after months of collaboration and discussion, the idea became a reality as an e-book on Amazon, where it quickly shot to the top of the charts as the number-one-selling e-book. There was no better platform to launch a new book than on the best Internet real estate program in the United States, *Secrets of Top Selling Agents*. We had the pleasure of having them both on our program.

Youtility is not just the name of *The New York Times* best-selling book by Jay Baer—it is also a concept. Baer explains the concept of *youtility* as, "Marketing so useful that people would actually pay for it." Although this may sound simple, there are very few companies and people who actually practice it. This is because many don't believe that providing information without getting something in return (business, a sale, etc.) is worth the time needed to invest. Baer shows readers why the practice of *youtility* can help you get more business and position yourself as an industry leader.

Baer discussed how being a marketer today is harder than ever. He brought up an example of television share percentage of the most popular programs from 1977 to today.

In 1977, *Happy Days* was the number one program on television, with a share (percentage of people with televisions watching) of 31.5. This meant that almost one-third of all American households were tuned in to watch the show. In 1987, the number one show was the *Cosby Show*. It had a 27.8 share. In 1997, *Seinfeld* was the king of television, with a 21.7 share. Ten years later, in 2007, *American Idol* was the leader with a 16.1 rating. Do you see a trend here? The viewer share decreased every decade for the most popular programs. It wasn't that the quality of programming had decreased (although some people may argue this point), it was the quantity of channel choices that dramatically increased over the years. In 1977, there were primarily three channels to choose from. By 2007, there were hundreds. Add mobile devices and computers into the mix, and marketing becomes exponentially more difficult.

After identifying the problem that marketers face, Baer discussed how consumers search for things today. He used his own recent home-buying experience as an example. Baer wanted to move his family to a Midwestern college town and, after doing some online research, saw that Bloomington, Indiana, was the best fit based on population, proximity to a major airport, quality of life, etc. Once he determined where he wanted to live, it was time to look for a home.

He began his online search for not just a new home, but a REALTOR® as well. He read through agent profile pages and reviews to help determine who he wanted to work with. After finding his agent, he began having her e-mail listings to him. The Baers eventually found their dream home and paid $1 million cash for it without ever physically visiting the home. Now that is putting a lot of trust in an agent! This trust was built on extensive research and communication. Although not all consumers conduct the same amount of research before making a buying decision, most will conduct at least some. And thanks to the Internet, conducting research has never been easier. It is critical for agents to be at the right place at the right time with their marketing and to make sure that their reputations are both promoted and protected.

REPUTATIONS ARE MADE IN REAL TIME

Your online reputation matters more than ever with the rise of review sites like Yelp and Google Reviews. Baer shared a hilarious (but actual—check it out on the *Secrets of Top Selling Agents* episode) Trip Advisor review about a motel he used to drive by every day while living in Flagstaff, Arizona. The review was so awful (yet funny) that it could destroy not only the reputation of the motel but also its future bookings and business. This can happen in any industry or profession, including real estate. Baer shared a recent study showing that 92 percent of Americans trust the advice and recommendations of family and friends, and that 79 percent trust online reviews. These powerful statistics remind us how important an online reputation is. Baer also said that only 47 percent of Americans trust advertising. Although the trust factor is low for advertising, it does create an enormous opportunity for those who are willing to fill the trust vacuum. This is where the concept of *youtility* comes into play.

SOCIAL MARKETING AND YOUTILITY

"The difference between the words 'help' and 'hype' is just two letters, but these two letters make all the difference in the world," Baer said. When it comes to marketing on social networks, brands are not only competing with each other, but also with the people consumers actually care about (family and friends). Baer discussed a personal experience he had recently when he logged into Facebook. The first four posts he saw were from his friend Dave, the Upland Brewing Company promoting a post, his wife, and the Wyoming Office of Tourism (one of Baer's clients). This is what marketers compete with every day across social networks. So how can companies and real estate professionals successfully compete in this space? By practicing *youtility*! Baer said that a common problem is that marketers spend a lot of time trying to be amazing with ads. This rarely works. Baer said marketers should focus on being useful instead.

Baer shared Hilton Hotels' social strategy both in his book and on *Secrets of Top Selling Agents*. Hilton has a Twitter handle called Hilton Suggests (@HiltonSuggests) that provides travelers with information about things to do in the city they are visiting. What is even more interesting is that @HiltonSuggests doesn't just help Hilton guests; it also provides great information to people staying at non-Hilton hotels. Why would they do this? Because by providing *youtility* now, Hilton is laying the foundation for these people's future hotel stays. Baer said that the next time these people decide to plan a trip, Hilton would probably be one of their top choices, thanks to the concept of *youtility*.

REAL ESTATE *YOUTILITY* EXAMPLES

Baer also pointed out two dynamic real estate *youtility* examples on *Secrets*. The Corcoran Group in New York (Barbara Corcoran's former company) sends out tweets from its Foursquare page about things to do in New York City when it is raining. It mentions everything from museums to restaurants, yet it does not ask consumers to view their listings. Why? Because the Corcoran Group is playing the long game in its quest for customer acquisition. Helping people in the city with great advice on where to eat and what to see positions them as experts on Manhattan, which becomes extremely useful when that same person decides to look for an apartment to rent or buy in the city. The Corcoran Group is laying the foundation for future business.

The second example was that of a Washington, DC, agent named Holli Beckman (@Apartmentalist). Beckman spends just five minutes per day on Twitter doing active prospecting. She searches for people who mention that they are looking to buy or rent in the DC area. How well have her efforts paid off so far? In only two months, she had written $150,000 in leases, and it was directly related to her five-minute-per-day Twitter prospecting strategy.

WE NEED MORE INFORMATION THAN EVER

Thanks to the Internet and Google, we can search for multiple pieces of information about a product or service in only a matter of seconds. Baer showed the audience on *Secrets* that in 2010, a person needed an average of 5.3 sources of information to make a decision. Just one year later, in 2011, a person needed 10.4 sources to make that same decision. Why did the sources needed double in only one year? It wasn't because people needed more data; it was because the Internet (and mobile) made it easier to access more information faster. The number of sources will continue to grow as information becomes progressively more readily available. Mobile usage doubled in 2013, which is a massive driver behind the ease with which consumers search for information online.

THE NEW RELATIONSHIP MODEL

The Internet has changed the way relationships are built today, according to Baer. On his webinar, he said that relationships are created with information first and people second. Going back to how he met his REALTOR® for his home purchase, he reminded the audience that he researched her first to learn as much about her as he could. Once he felt confident that she was the best match for him and his family, he contacted her. He also showed how practicing *youtility* could be a massive lead generator in your local community, illustrating his point with the story of Taxi Mike.

Banff, Alberta, Canada, is a ski town. When people go there to visit, they naturally want to know where the best places to eat, drink, and have fun are. Enter Taxi Mike, a cab driver who practices *youtility*. Each quarter, Taxi Mike puts out his dining guide (called *Taxi Mike's Dining Guide*) and places his much-in-demand brochures in hotels, bars, restaurants, and other businesses, for both locals and tourists to take. Why does Taxi Mike spend so much time publishing a dining guide? It is because he knows that being useful pays off. After people go out to the places he recommends, who do you think they will call for a ride home? Taxi Mike. Baer said that Taxi Mike's dining guide has become so popular in Banff that he has become a local celebrity. Locals and tourists alike have asked Taxi Mike to take pictures with them and sign their dining guides.

Think about how you can take Taxi Mike's example and practice *youtility* in your community. You probably know more about the parks, restaurants, neighborhoods, schools, and shops than the average person. Although you might not create a Taxi Mike style-dining guide, you could create a blog and do an individual post about each of your favorite places and what makes them special. When people look to buy a home, they are looking at the community as much as (if not more than) the home itself. If they can find you during their online search and be educated and entertained by your blog posts, why wouldn't they contact you to help them find a home? You have already shown them through your blog that you are an expert about the area. Perception is reality, and you are perceived as the expert. Baer stresses this by saying to teach better (via informational blogs or social posts, for example) and sell more. Focus less on trying to be the "best REALTOR®" and more on being the best teacher about your area. If you do this, you will make more money. It has been proven time and again.

OFFLINE *YOUTILITY* FOR REAL ESTATE IDEAS

Although Taxi Mike also has a website (www.TaxiMike.com), his dining guide is primarily known as being an offline *youtility*. Offline *youtility* can still work in real estate as well, and Baer lists a few examples on the webinar. Mini American yard flags, for example, are great around Memorial Day and the Fourth of July. In addition to being a nice tool for your geographic farm, they will also most likely be kept and displayed somewhere in that person's home or yard.

Baer also displayed an example of an agent who gives away small pine trees to potential clients, complete with planting and caring instructions. These instructions invite the person to request more free trees and inform him or her that the agent has been in the community for years and has expert knowledge on the real estate in the area.

A third example Baer brought up is how many real estate companies are now opening coffee shops next to or within their buildings. Because many people already enjoy the idea of meeting up for a cup of coffee, these savvy offices are bringing the coffee shops in-house. This is a great icebreaker with buyers and sellers, especially when negotiating contracts or terms. A coffee shop makes the meeting seem more casual and laid-back than a traditional real estate meeting and can facilitate better connections between agents and their clients. OCF Realty in Philadelphia is a company that is already doing this with much success, according to Baer.

MANAGING THE SALES FUNNEL

Baer discussed the three segments that comprise the sales funnel in business. They are simply named the top of the funnel, the middle of the funnel, and the bottom of the funnel. Each segment serves its own purpose in attracting and converting sales customers.

Top of the funnel. The top of the sales funnel is where customers go to get a broad range of questions answered. This is usually the beginning of their search. In real estate, this might be a question about an area, community, or lifestyle. Baer brought up two good examples of companies that have strong top-of-funnel sales: TheCassinaGroup.com and NakedPhilly.com. NakedPhilly.com is owned by OCF Realty, which is the same company that owns the coffee shop next to their office. It is so popular with customers that it gets more web traffic than all the real estate blogs in Philadelphia combined!

Campbell Byrum added how her team at Homes.com took the concept of the sales funnel and applied it to the consumer-facing side of Homes.com. She started by gathering her team for brainstorming sessions in which they could define various personas of Homes.com and ForRent.com users. Then, based on the information they gathered, they put their top-of-the-funnel plan into place. They made Homes.com and ForRent.com's blogs more robust than ever and developed an idea gallery for consumers. They came up with entertaining, decorating, holiday, and other popular ideas that were located at the top of the sales funnel. They also produced Twitter Chats about the buying and selling process to help educate consumers.

Middle of the funnel. The middle of the sales funnel goes deeper into information about a product or service. In real estate, this might mean being somewhat specific about properties, amenities, and features. Baer showed an example on *Secrets of Top*

Selling Agents of a Seattle-based team (www.TacomaJones.com) effectively using the middle of the funnel. He illustrated how they decentralize their *youtility* by taking their videos to multiple mediums and by displaying a deeper focus on local schools, property types, etc.

Campbell Byrum then discussed her team's middle-of-funnel strategy. They realized that true *youtility* isn't just about pushing a blog post, but rather taking that post and pairing it with similar posts to develop an e-guide. The guide would be much more useful to consumers than just a single post. They also focused on the power and reach of infographics to better inform consumers about the buying and selling process. Once these middle-of-funnel ideas became reality, Campbell Byrum's team would then do a paid advertising spend on social media to promote their e-guides and infographics. This proved to be much more effective than just promoting a single blog post.

Bottom of the funnel. When consumers get to the bottom of the sales funnel, they are looking for very specific information about the product or service. These types of questions might be about the buying process or specific costs and expenses related to buying a home. Real estate professionals can connect with bottom-of-funnel consumers by writing a blog post or responding via e-mail to answer a question about the buying or selling process. Baer told a great story of bottom-of-funnel success with a Virginia company named River Pools & Spas.

During the Great Recession, the last thing many people were thinking about was having a pool installed in their yards. Most were struggling just to make their mortgage payments. River Pools & Spas quickly realized that if they didn't change their way of thinking, they would be out of business. Owner Marcus Sheridan and his partners brainstormed to find ways to reach customers creatively by thinking "outside the box." They knew that whatever it was they decided on had to be very inexpensive (they didn't have the revenue to use for new marketing) but effective— not exactly an easy thing to do. They thought about the customer experience and some of the common problems or questions their customers typically had during the sales process. Marcus decided to put himself in customers' shoes and think about what they might do before purchasing a pool. His experience taught him that buyers typically had questions—lots of them. He decided to write out every possible question he could think of that his customers had asked him in the past. Then he spent his nights and weekends writing out the answers to all the questions. After answering all these questions, he posted them on his company's website for consumers to view and read. He had now turned his website into a *youtility*. The results were stunning. His close rate skyrocketed to 80 percent (if a customer read at least thirty questions on his site), as opposed to the industry average of only 10 percent. His SEO on Google was a powerful lead generator for River Pool & Spas, but it wasn't because of a paid advertising campaign. You see, when people went on Google to get their specific pool question answered, River Pool & Spas usually appeared first because it had the answer on its website. Also, 80 percent of River Pools & Spas sales were done without a sales call. Consumers already had the answers to their questions, because they read them on the River Pools & Spas website. They didn't want to even look anywhere else, because Marcus's company had done such a great job of positioning itself as the industry leader.

Baer also mentioned Raj Qsar (chapter 5 in this book) and how he is using his website to capture bottom-of-funnel sales leads. The Boutique Real Estate Group's website (www.TBREG. com) is packed with videos of prior work, as well as what sellers can expect in terms of marketing and advertising if they list with them.

Campbell Byrum also discussed how her team improved the bottom of the funnel at Homes.com, where every month millions of consumers visit to buy, sell, or rent a home. This was accomplished by improving the home values channel on the site (where neighborhoods can be searched to discover their homes' estimated value) and by improving the content on the listing detail pages by making the estimated mortgage rates easier to understand, adding a mortgage calculator, and having an "explore the neighborhood" feature built into the page. Providing this level of *youtility* definitely has improved the bottom-of-funnel sales experience for consumers on Homes.com.

FINAL THOUGHTS FROM JAY BAER

One of the problems Baer has noticed with people trying to become more useful is that they try to schedule time to do it. To this, Baer offered some advice: "Think of *youtility* as a river that constantly flows rather than a lake you have to schedule to visit." He says you cannot schedule greatness in your work. It is something that just happens. He said REALTORS® should focus on blogging and video blogging at the local level to capture leads from the sales-funnel process. One piece of advice he stressed was directed toward agents who had trouble finding neighborhood and mortgage data online. He encouraged them to borrow the data from Homes.com and to use that information in their blog posts. This will save agents time while also giving them accurate data to help capture more bottom-of-the-funnel leads.

Start achieving your *youtility* goals and discover *Why Smart Real Estate Professionals are Helping, Not Selling* when you purchase Baer and Campbell Byrum's eBook, *Youtility for Real Estate* on Amazon.com. You can also visit ConvinceandConvert.com to connect with Baer's team of consulting and social media specialists to "create more customers and keep the ones you've already earned."

Eight
Jimmy Mackin

@JimmyMackin

Inbox Zero

Jimmy Mackin has been called the "Mark Zuckerberg" of the digital real estate industry. The wunderkind has been at the forefront of social media and marketing for the real estate industry since being a guest speaker and contributor for Inman News. Named to the Inman "Most Influential 100" list numerous times because of his social-media and technology prowess, Mackin founded two of the most popular Facebook groups in real estate: *What Should I Spend My Money On?* and *Tech Support Groups for Real Estate Agents.* He currently spends his time at Curaytor, the company he cofounded with Chris Smith (chapters 6 and 12 in this book). Together they have established a loyal following of some of the top real estate agents and teams in the United States.

I met Mackin at an Agent Reboot conference at which I was also speaking. I wanted to verify a slide in my presentation that contained a direct quote from him. We hit it off from there. I was impressed by how intrigued he was about our social-media management product, and we continued our conversations at each successive conference. Deb has always looked for great contributors for *Secrets of Top Selling Agents*, so I put her in contact with Mackin to arrange his first appearance on the program.

Mackin was such a popular guest on the show that he has returned for additional episodes. His *Secrets* popularity wasn't just coming from REALTORS® and brokers, however. Homes. com was so impressed with Mackin's knowledge and web presence that he was a featured speaker at the Homes.com Education Theater at the National Association of REALTORS® convention from 2012 to 2014.

In April 2013, Mackin appeared on *Secrets of Top Selling Agents* to discuss how agents could go to "Inbox Zero." The episode focused on how agents could better manage their e-mail using powerful apps and tools, many of which are still relatively unused today.

REALTORS® are addicted to e-mail. In fact, the average worker spends 2.1 hours per day on their e-mail alone. REALTORS® are no different than the average worker. Agents spend hours every day reading and responding to e-mails. Although this may be a necessary part of your business, it doesn't have to take over your life. Mackin said this is where agents need to set boundaries with their clients. For example, sending an e-mail to a client at an abnormal time is a big mistake, according to Mackin. It may not seem like a big deal, but it subconsciously tells the client that the agent is available at all times. If the client sends another late-night e-mail a week later, he or she will be upset if the agent doesn't respond right away. Once the agent sets a precedent, it is hard to reset it. The lesson here is not to be a slave to your clients. Your doctor or accountant will probably not return your calls or e-mails late at night. Why should you be an exception?

THE FIVE OPTIONS OF E-MAIL

Merlin Mann created the concept of Inbox Zero in 2007, according to Mackin. Mann found that when someone received an e-mail message, there were five things he or she could do with it:

1. Delete it.
2. Delegate it to someone else.
3. Respond to it.
4. Defer it until later.
5. Complete the task required by the e-mail.

Which option do you most associate your e-mail habits with?

INBOX BANKRUPTCY

When individuals or businesses get in over their heads financially and can no longer afford to make all their payments, bankruptcy becomes a viable option. But what happens when a person neglects his or her e-mail accounts for days or even weeks? They may consider declaring inbox bankruptcy. Mackin explained when and why to do this.

Mackin said that if an agent has one thousand or more unread e-mails, it could take quite a while to go through them. He said it might be best to clear them all. This doesn't necessarily mean deleting every message, but maybe archiving them instead. He then advised agents to look at the last two to three days and respond to everything (or delete if the e-mail is junk mail). Most of the older messages are too stale at this point to respond to, so you don't have to open them unless they are very important.

GMAIL IS BEST

Mackin focused on Gmail during his *Secrets* episode because it is his personal favorite platform. There are so many things we can do with Gmail. Mackin pointed out some cool features, one being the ability to have a branded e-mail account. This is great for any small-business owner or independent broker who wants to have an e-mail account branded to his or her company name. Gmail is also cloud-based and an open platform, which encourages third-party developers to design apps that plug into Gmail. The following are some other great features that Mackin mentioned on *Secrets*.

Step 1: Setting up your Gmail inbox. This is the first step to getting yourself to *inbox zero*. In Gmail, click on the gear in the upper-right corner, then click on "Settings." Under the "General" tab, go to "Send and Archive" and select "Show 'Send & Archive' button in reply."

Now it is time to set up your labels.

Step 2: Setting up your labels. In "Settings," under "Labels" tab create a specific label (folder) for each person/client you are currently working with. Once you have created a label or folder (Gmail calls them "labels"), you can then create a new filter for that label. Under "Filters" tab click on "Create a New Filter," select a client's email address then apply that client's Label, so you can easily access all e-mail from them.

Mackin gave the viewing audience (and you should do this as well) a homework assignment to improve their Gmail skills. He encouraged each audience member to get in front of his or her computer and to set up a label (folder) and filter for each client. He then said to create a filter for Facebook notification e-mails. Use the upper-right drop-down menu in an unwanted e-mail and then choose"filter messages like this" and select the "Skip the inbox" option. Repeat this sequence for each social-media site you belong to.

Step 3: How to forward e-mails from other e-mail accounts to Gmail. As a working professional, you probably have multiple e-mail accounts. It is bad enough that the average worker spends more than two hours per day writing, reading, and responding to e-mails, but having to do this over multiple accounts will only further complicate things. "The solution," Mackin said, "is to organize e-mail from all accounts into one inbox." Here is how you can forward your e-mails to Gmail:

1. Go to Gear>"Settings">"Accounts" tab
2. Click "Add a Mail Account"
3. Enter your e-mail and password.

E-mail will now be forwarded to your Gmail account.

AWESOME GOOGLE APPS

Another great feature about Gmail is the applications that are built for the platform. These apps can be added to your Gmail account from the Google Chrome store. Mackin discussed three of his personal favorites in his *Secrets* webinar:

Unroll.me. This free app helps streamline your e-mail by reviewing all e-mails received and determining which messages were sent by a computer (often spam). These e-mails are then rolled up into a single e-mail. Simply open the daily roll-up e-mail from Unroll.me to review all these computer-generated messages. You can then decide which e-mails are good and which are junk and can easily unsubscribe from e-mails you don't want. Mackin said he had 114 e-mails in one roll-up. This saved him from going through 25,000 e-mails in one year! Unroll.me is a great asset if you truly want to get to *inbox zero*.

Yesware. Yesware is an e-mail tracking app that has both a free (limited tracked e-mails) and premium (a ton of options) version. It allows an e-mail sender to use such functions as attach read receipts to e-mails (so that the recipient acknowledges that the message has been read) and track when and how often an e-mail message was opened. Being able to see when your e-mail was opened can be very powerful in any sales position, but even more powerful for REALTORS®. If you send a drip campaign or listings to a prospect and then see when it was opened, you could "happen to call" that person within a few minutes of the message being opened, when the message's content is still at the top of the prospect's mind. Watch your lead conversion rate skyrocket! Mail tracking from Yesware can assist in this greatly.

Boomerang. Boomerang is a Google plug-in app that allows a sender's e-mail to be returned to him or her if it is not opened. All the sender has to do is to check the Boomerang box before sending the message, and then determine the length of time before the e-mail is returned to the sender.

SMARTPHONE MAIL APPS

In addition to the Yesware app, Mackin also recommended Mailbox, an app owned by Dropbox. Mailbox enables users to better manage their e-mails from their smartphones with both traditional methods (archiving and deleting) and some really cool ones such as reminder messages sent to the user to reply to a message. Mailbox also allows users to develop custom actions as well. Best of all, it syncs with Gmail, both on mobile devices and desktop computers.

Jimmy Mackin is a wealth of knowledge with social media, but his *Inbox Zero Secrets* webinar gave a step-by-step strategy for how REALTORS® can better organize their e-mails, close more deals, and get their lives back.

Once you've taken control of your inbox, visit Curaytor.com to learn how Curaytor can help you reach and engage with the right audience on Facebook. Curaytor's techniques can help you direct more traffic to your website, connect with more qualified leads, and close more sales.

Nine

Tom Ferry

@TomFerry

The Rich and the Rest

Tom Ferry is the most in-demand real estate coach today. As CEO of Tom Ferry International, Ferry was named the number one real estate educator in the Swanepoel Power 200 Index for four consecutive years and has one of the largest social media audiences in the industry. The results speak for themselves: he has been featured in *The New York Times* and has helped more than five hundred thousand agents throughout his career. His current real estate clients average $372,000 per year in gross commission income. He is also the best-selling author of *Life! By Design*.

We can credit Deb Helleren with the outstanding effort to snag Ferry and his wealth of knowledge for the *Secrets of Top Selling Agents* episode. He appeared on our May 2015 broadcast. We knew he would bring his passion, knowledge, and following to the program. His episode discussed how the rich differentiate themselves from the rest of the pack. He wanted to illustrate how today's REALTORS® can adopt the same traits to propel themselves into this elite category.

THE NUMBER ONE QUESTION

The most popular question REALTORS® are asked is, "How's the market?" Ferry took this question a step further on *Secrets*. He asked the audience how the market in their heads was, meaning how they felt the market would be for them in the current year. He then asked the audience if they were focused on attracting listings. Then he set the tone for the rest of his message by displaying real estate's rich and the rest, according to NAR statistics. In 2014:

- 1 percent of REALTORS® made more than $1 million.
- 5 percent of REALTORS® made more than $250,000.
- 21 percent of REALTORS® made more than $100,000.
- 54 percent of REALTORS® made less than $50,000.

He followed these statistics by asking the audience where they wanted to be with their income level. Although almost anyone would say they want to be rich, Ferry asked if they knew how to get to the level they desired. Did they even know what the top 5 percent of agents do differently than them? Ferry asked, "What if you did more of what the rich do in their businesses? What would happen to your income?"

CHARACTERISTICS OF THE RICH

Top agents don't become and stay immensely successful by accident. They possess characteristics that most agents fail to capitalize on. The rich focus on closing the inefficiency gaps in their business. Top-producing agents not only use the following characteristics; they master them. According to Ferry top agents:

- Have an organized database.
- Contact the people in their database.
- Do consistent marketing to their database.
- Maintain multiple online lead-generation sources.
- Practice geographic farming.
- Hone open-house conversion skills.
- Stay current on the latest trends and technologies.
- Hire a competent staff.
- Generate niche listings.
- Keep business systems and checklists.
- Generate listing appointments.
- Are able to convert listing appointments into clients.
- Generate buyer appointments.
- Have a mindset for success.

Ferry and his team conducted a survey with REALTORS®. While it revealed many interesting statistics, there was one that stood out: 40 percent of agents surveyed were not using a CRM system. There is absolutely no way an agent can scale his or her business to the top 5 percent of agents without one. You must have a CRM system to take your business to the next level.

YOUR WHY IS JUST AS IMPORTANT AS YOUR WHAT OR HOW

"When branding a business, the rich focus on growth," Ferry said. He then identified the five phases of business.

Phase 1: Start-up
- New business
- Developing systems
- Trial and error

Phase 2: Growth
- Hitting stride
- Scaling the business

Phase 3: Cash cow
- Company is peaking

Phase 4: Fading winner
- Still doing well but declining slowly
- Need to go back to growth stage

Phase 5: Restructure
- Business needs to adapt to changing environment
- Need to go back to growth stage

Ferry said the key to growth is consistency. The rich are consistent with their systems; the rest are not. The rich develop turnkey, relevant lead-generation systems and have great conversion rates compared with the rest of the industry. The rich continually focus on marketing; the rest do not. Ferry quoted Peter Drucker in the webinar, saying, "All business is marketing and innovation."

"The moment you stop innovating and marketing," Ferry said, "you are out of the game." The key is to focus on doing it better and on growth. "The rich and the rest both *hate* to do what it takes to be successful," according to Ferry. "The difference is that the rich do it anyway, and the rest do not."

LEAD GENERATION

Lead generation is the lifeblood of a REALTOR'S® business. It keeps the pipeline flowing. Ferry broke this segment of *Secrets of Top Selling Agents* into three sections: lead-generation systems, lead-generation formulas, and lead-generation sources.

Lead generation systems. This was perhaps the biggest eye-opener for the audience. Ferry said the rich not only have better lead-conversion rates than the rest; they also have more sources of leads coming in. In his experience, Ferry has found that struggling agents have only one to three lead-generation sources. Fewer sources means fewer opportunities. Good agents have between four and six lead-generation sources. Ferry said the top agents have *more than ten* different lead-generation sources.

Lead-generation formula. Like all successful businesses, agents need to set goals for themselves. Ferry said you have to know your numbers. He offered a formula for setting and reaching your annual goal:

Step 1: Define your goal: houses you want to sell.
Step 2: Multiply your goal by fifty contacts.

Step 3: Divide this number by ten months (factor in vacation and down time).

Step 4: Divide this number by twenty-four days (the number of days you will work in a month).

This is the part where many agents get stuck because they lose the motivation to be consistent with their formula. Ferry said to ask yourself, "What's my motivation today?" But when you ask yourself this question, look at your motivation. Is it a photo of your kids? Your spouse? Your family? This is what keeps the rich going strong every day.

Lead-generation sources. It's very simple—if an agent wants to elevate himself or herself to the top 5 percent of all agents, he or she needs more sources of lead generation. Ferry identified the seven most popular sources used by the top 5 percent of REALTORS®:

1. Database management and referrals (Ferry said the average consumer moves every ten years).
2. Geographic farming (Ferry suggested watching his show, the #TomFerryShow to learn more about this).
3. Open houses.
4. Direct mail.
5. Expired listings.
6. For Sale by Owner listings (FSBOs).
7. Advertising.

Ferry said that while lead generation is important, it is only the beginning of the relationship between an agent and his or her client. Although 80 percent of agents say they need leads, only 20 percent of agents actually focus on lead conversion. Converting the leads is where top agents stand out and get rich.

LEAD-GENERATION STRATEGIES

Mega open houses. Ferry recommended having a private lunch and inviting only the neighbors to it. Neighbors always want to see a local house for sale (to compare it to theirs), but the value here is in connecting with these people. Ferry said that after one house sells on a block, one or two others will usually come up for sale soon after. An open-house luncheon is a great opportunity to connect with these potential sellers and get the inside track on their business.

Old, old expired listings. Many markets are white-hot today, with multiple offers coming in on a house as soon as it hits the market. Although most expired listings get worked over by multiple agents, there are many homes that went up for sale during the Great Recession that didn't sell and have never been relisted. Ferry suggested sending a postcard to these people (or door knocking) to ask if they would like to know what their home is worth now. Many will be pleasantly surprised by how much their houses have appreciated during this period. Very few agents are working these types of listings.

Texting strategy. Ferry recommended two actions to generate more listings from referrals using a texting strategy. How powerful is text marketing? He said that 95 percent of text messages are responded to within five minutes.

Text strategy 1: "Hi, (name). Home values have really improved, and I was curious, have you had any thoughts of selling?"

If they answer no, you can follow up with, "Curious about your home's value?"

If they answer yes, follow up with, "Wonderful! I'll put together your home's value. Have you done any upgrades? Once it's ready, do you want to meet for coffee, or shall I e-mail it to you?"

Text strategy 2: Ask one of three questions:

1. "Have you had any thoughts of selling?"
2. "Do you know anyone who's had thoughts of selling?"
3. "Do you know anyone who tried to sell in the past and it didn't work out?"

If they answer that they are considering selling or are not really thinking about it (they very well might be), Ferry offered this follow-up text: "At what price would you become a seller?" You would be surprised at how many people answer this question.

HOW TO DOMINATE YOUR COMMUNITY

Dominating your community's real estate market isn't rocket science, but there is a science to it. Ferry laid out the process on *Secrets*. He called it his "Geo-Farming Domination Plan."

Step 1. Map your track record of sales using Google Maps or Batchgeo. This will give you a great visual image showing where the bulk of your sales have taken place. It also displays your sales in a beautiful, mapped-out illustration (Ferry showed a great example on *Secrets*).

Step 2. Where is the annual turnover rate higher than 6 percent in your area? This is the big issue, according to Ferry.

"You don't fish where there are no fish," Ferry said. If turnover is less than 6 percent in a given area, you should look to expand your farm or try a different subdivision where the turnover rate is higher.

Step 3. How many houses can you effectively manage in your farm? Managing means asking yourself if you have the budget and other resources to effectively market yourself to your selected geo-farmed region consistently throughout the year.

Step 4. What's your budget (sweat equity or check equity)? If you have a low budget, Ferry recommended putting in more "sweat equity," meaning that you work your farm by going door-to-door, meeting your prospects face-to-face, and personally giving them marketing materials.

Step 5. Does your company offer incentives for farming? Partnerships? Ask your manager or real estate partners, such as mortgage brokers or title companies, for assistance in paying for your marketing materials and postage.

SEVEN CAMPAIGNS TO DOMINATE

Once you have selected your farm, it is time to put together your marketing campaigns. Ferry offered seven different types of campaigns that can dominate your competition in your farm.

1. **Direct mail.** Many people thought that e-mail would kill the direct-mail business. Most REALTORS® don't send snail mail anymore, which is why you can stand out in your market by doing so. Ferry recommended mailing out one to two pieces per month, and he showed some actual examples of lead-generating pieces on *Secrets*. They

are simple but powerful, and they speak directly to the consumer with a strong message.

2. **Door knocking/door drops.** "Courage equals rewards," Ferry said on *Secrets of Top Selling Agents.* Most agents are not comfortable doing this, which makes it a prime opportunity for an ambitious agent to personally get to know the prospects in his or her farm.

3. **Mega open houses.** As mentioned earlier in this chapter.

4. **Google pay-per-click.** "This is always a good idea," Ferry said.

5. **Expired listings (old and new) and FSBOs:** Ferry discussed his technique for old, expired listings earlier in this chapter and talks more about this topic on his *Secrets* episode.

6. **Community functions.** See and be seen in your community.

7. **Notice of defaults.** This is an opportunity to get in front of struggling homeowners and help them make the best decision for their future.

TECHNOLOGY

Technology plays a huge role in savvy marketing today, and Ferry is on the cutting-edge of it. He discussed some of his favorite marketing ideas using some of the latest technology to "push the envelope."

- **Online advertising.** Get yourself seen and capture leads on the most popular portals, such as Homes.com.
- **Facebook advertising.** Create ads to grow audience size (page likes) or to generate leads (e.g., home values).

- **Google pay-per-click.**
- **Video marketing.** "Agents who do this correctly are killing it," Ferry said. "Bring your swagger!"
- **E-mail marketing.** For example, drip marketing campaigns.
- **Text marketing (especially for follow-up).** "An absolute must for every agent," Ferry said.

Tom Ferry recapped his webinar by reinforcing to the audience his point about the difference between the best agents and the mediocre ones. The rich have a better mindset of how they approach their careers. The rich dream bigger, and Ferry challenged the audience to set a bigger goal for the next twelve months, because "that's what the rich do." Finally, the rich have a plan, meaning a detailed business plan of how they will continue to grow their businesses. Ferry concluded by challenging the audience to "Do something today that your future self will thank you for." Great advice from a great teacher.

Take charge of your business, make bigger goals, and achieve them with the tips you find in *Life! By Design: 6 Steps to an Extraordinary You*. This hands-on guide by coaching legend Tom Ferry is available at TomFerry.com and will help you design and balance your ideal life.

Ten

Kelly Mitchell

@KellyMitchell

Seven Ways to Find Your Niche and Own It

To say that Kelly Mitchell is an influencer in real estate would be a massive understatement. A former Hawaiian REALTOR®, Mitchell spoke nationally at real estate events and is a serial entrepreneur. Since 2015, Mitchell has jumped industries and now spends her time vlogging and storytelling about the wine lifestyle on TheWineSiren.com as well as contributing to the Huffington Post.

While in real estate she created the popular podcast Agent Caffeine. She was recognized multiple times on both the Inman "100 Most Influential" people in real estate and the Swanepoel Power 200 (ranked 8). She cowrote *The Swanepoel Technology Report* and was a contributor to the best-selling book *Real: A Potion to Passion, Purpose, and Profits in Real Estate.*

We had Mitchell as a guest on our June 2014 broadcast of *Secrets of Top Selling Agents.* Deb Helleren made the connection with Mitchell, and she was delighted to be on the program. Based on her vast experience in the real estate industry, Mitchell wanted to do a program to stress the importance of having a niche in the real estate industry and how it could help agents differentiate themselves from the other agents in their market. Her *Secrets* webinar was a road map to show agents how they can discover their niche, and own it as well.

WHAT IS A NICHE?

Mitchell knows how to carve out and own a niche. She currently hosts two podcast programs that focus on entrepreneurs. Her passion is obvious, but how she differentiates herself from others is her tie-ins to coffee (*Agent Caffeine*) and wine (*The Wine Siren*). Her tagline for Agent Caffeine is "It's all about the buzz." Do you see the double meaning in the word "buzz?" The tagline for The Wine Siren is "Wine soaked adventures from Napa to Provence". It is this consistency in her branding and niche that have enabled her to have such a loyal and large following. She would not have the following she has today if she tried to be all things to all people. Focusing on entrepreneurship makes her stand out.

Mitchell said a niche is a specialized but profitable corner of the market. It is something you are passionate about. It is an element of your personal brand, and it makes your business more memorable to your clients and prospects. The key is to first identify your niche—then dominate it.

Mitchell provided some characteristics to consider when searching for your niche in the market. First you need to identify a specific segment of the market. Maybe it is foreclosures, for example, or a city or county. "Whatever you choose, it must be distinct," Mitchell said. Your niche needs to be specialized. You probably have heard the saying "A jack-of-all-trades but master of none." A niche is specialized, which will make you a master of a particular segment of the market. Many agents get nervous about "limiting" themselves to a niche because they think they will lose business by focusing only on a segment of the total market. Mitchell said every agent can work with all types of buyers and sellers, but how many can dominate a targeted audience? Not many. If someone is looking for foreclosure properties to buy, they will feel much more comfortable with a "foreclosure specialist" than with someone who knows only a little about them.

WHY CHOOSE A NICHE?

The vast majority of real estate professionals do not specialize in a particular area of real estate. They try to be all things to all people. But how can they stand out if they practice this type of business? They can't. This is why you need to have a niche.

Having a niche makes a powerful first (and lasting) impression with people. It is powerful because it defines your passion. You don't have to fake it or pretend, and clients notice these things. They will remember you better because you are a specialist. A niche will also enable you to create a perception of what you do and how you do it. This is a perfect way to capture "top of mind" awareness for future proposals and client referrals. This is what will separate you from your competition.

FINDING YOUR NICHE

To identify a niche you can enjoy and make money specializing in, Mitchell said to ask yourself the following questions:

1. "What am I passionate about?" You have to love what you do.
2. "If I weren't working right now, what would I be doing?" This can help you identify your true passions, which you can then tie to real estate.
3. "What am I most excited about and/or interested in?" What will make you want to get up and go to work every day?
4. "Who is my ideal client?"
5. "If I could be anything or anyone in the world, who would I be?"
6. "When I read, what kind of books or articles are most compelling to me?"
7. "How can these interests interact with my business? Where are the communities or compliments?"

HOW NOT TO BE A JACK-OF-ALL-TRADES

The biggest challenge for agents is that most want to be all things to all people because they feel that that is the only way to make money in business. What happens is actually the opposite. "We become a whole lot of nothing," Mitchell said. Too many agents make this critical error, causing themselves, in the end, more harm than good. Mitchell offered seven steps to selecting your niche on her *Secrets* episode.

1. **Choose smaller because it's better.** Having a specialized niche can pay off in a big way. Mitchell gave an example of an agent whose divorce experience transformed her into a divorce-sale specialist. While this may seem like a very small segment, specializing in it has proved lucrative for the agent. (Since half of all marriages end in divorce, this should not be surprising.) Thinking smaller has become better and more profitable.

2. **Define, then focus.** You can't just "sort of" have a niche. You have to first define what your niche is and what it encompasses. Once you define your niche, it is time to focus on your game plan for how you are going to market yourself.

3. **Envision your ideal customer for your niche.** Who are your core customers? How will they be able to find you?

4. **Make yourself irresistible to those who share the same interests.** How will you stand out? By working with clients who are passionate about the same things. This is how you make yourself irresistible to clients.

5. **Find the need, differentiate yourself, and fill it.** Where is the void in your market? How can you fill it? Differentiate yourself from your competition. What will you do differently than everyone else? Mitchell said one

way to refine your niche is to seek feedback from clients. Their opinions matter and can help you become a better agent. Do not neglect this very important step.

6. **When looking for a niche, think about your own experiences.** Your real-life experiences cannot be replaced by reading books. These experiences are education from the real world. They can be invaluable in identifying your niche.

7. **Create the message of your niche, and run with it.** Once you find a niche, create a tagline or message about why you own it. Then build your business plan around it. You are now building the foundation.

But why would someone work with you just because you specialize in a particular area of real estate? Because they want to work with the best! Mitchell identified other reasons to become a niche REALTOR®:

- Doing business with those like us is easier.
- You have similar interests.
- Business is more enjoyable—it is easier to bond and build rapport.
- Your communication styles are often the same.
- You become more confident.
- You become an authority in your niche.
- You will attract others like you and generate more referrals.
- People like to work with like-minded people.

NICHE IDEAS

Mitchell gave some traditional and nontraditional ideas for agents to find and choose their niches. Mitchell doesn't like to call traditional niches "defined" ones. She prefers calling them "target niches." She said almost every agent works inside some degree of some or all of the traditional niches. She challenged the viewers to ask themselves how they will stand out. It is possible to do so.

Traditional Niches

- Distressed/foreclosures/short sales
- Investors
- First-time buyers
- Sellers
- Property type marketing (luxury, condo, vacation, second home, waterfront, etc.)
- Age targeting
- Location, location, location (neighborhood, town, city)

Emotionally Targeted Traditional Niches

- Lifestyle (LGBT, metrosexual, luxury, foodie)
- Hobbies (hunting, fishing, sailing)
- Interests (sports, architecture, design)
- Location (neighborhood expert)
- Workplace (relocation, corporate housing, military housing)
- Life stage (age fifty-five-plus expert, millennial)

To really stand out, however, Mitchell recommends combining a traditional niche with a nontraditional niche or focusing on a unique niche individually. Here are examples of the nontraditional niches Mitchell discussed in her *Secrets* webinar.

Nontraditional Niches

- The Zen agent
- The connector agent
- The social-media-expert agent
- The thespian agent
- The all-pro-athlete agent
- The digital-media agent
- The tech-expert agent
- The event-PR agent

CREATING THE MAGIC

It is not always easy to find your specialty. If it were, everyone would be doing it. It takes passion, self-analysis, and an inner drive to want to be known for it. Discovery and development of your personal brand are some of the most important things you can do to create and refine your niche.

Mitchell said that to create the magic in your niche, you must understand these facts:

- Being unique is required.
- A niche is just one part of your business.
- Your personal brand is directly related to it.
- Your passion will drive your business.

OWNING YOUR NICHE

Finding and creating your niche is not the end of your journey, but the beginning. You now have to dedicate your business marketing to owning your niche. This is how your core clients will find and refer you to others. Mitchell offered seven ideas for how you can own your niche:

1. **Add it to your website**—Add your specialty on the "About Me" page, and discuss why you are the expert.
2. **Include it in your social networks**—Create a business or community page around it.
3. **Use it on your e-mail**—Add it to your e-mail signature.
4. **Print it on your business cards**—Put it on your business cards.
5. **Add it to your voicemail**—Mention it on your voicemail.
6. **Tell people about it**—Start with your sphere and other centers of influence.
7. **Show your passion**—Love what you do; live what you love.

FINAL THOUGHTS FROM KELLY MITCHELL

Mitchell concluded her *Secrets* episode by asking listeners to imagine themselves on their deathbeds. What do you want to be known for at the end of your life? How were you different from everyone else? Did your passion show in your work? "If you can think about your niche in these terms," Mitchell said, "you will not only find your niche, but you will own it as well."

Embracing your passions and incorporating them into your business is a great way to create and own your niche. Mitchell has expanded her wine lovers' niche to the next level by starting WineSiren.com. In 2017, she was also ranked "14th International Wine Influencer."

Eleven

Bob Corcoran

@BobCorcoran1

Ten Best Practices for Converting Online Leads

Bob Corcoran is one of the real estate industry's leading consultants and coaches. His company, Corcoran Consulting and Coaching, focuses on performance coaching and business systems for real estate agents, brokers, and companies. He has a passionate and loyal following of successful agents who consistently rank in *The Wall Street Journal*'s top 250 agents in the United States, and has been one of the most in-demand speakers at conferences and trade shows for years. He's also been named to the prestigious Inman News "100 Most Influential" people in real estate. His company is located in southern Illinois.

I first met Bob Corcoran in Las Vegas in 2012. I was asked to speak at his Corcoran Conference and was blown away by how passionate he was. I thought I had a lot of energy when I spoke, but Corcoran is not only passionate and energizing but also very convincing. When he talks, people listen. He has built a loyal following on proven results and a powerful system, and his clients will make sure to tell you that. Every time I see Corcoran, I can guarantee two things: he will be the best-dressed person in the room, and he will always be laser-focused. I have never seen him any other way, and I think that the consistency of his appearance and message has been key to his success. Corcoran has been a friend of *Secrets of Top Selling Agents* producers Mel McMurrin and Deb Helleren for years, having done multiple *Secrets* episodes, but it was his webinar on converting online leads that created a major buzz and registration rush for the episode. The ten tips he discussed on *Secrets* and in the following pages could mean the difference between having an incredible year and having a merely good year.

LEAD GENERATION IS EASY

Almost any REALTOR® who has generated online leads over the years will tell you that generating the leads is the easy part. There are many places to get leads. Corcoran knows this firsthand; he has heard the same story from thousands of agents over the years. "The problem," Corcoran said, "is managing and converting the leads." This is where many agents fail. Whether it is because they are too slow to respond or fail to follow up properly, many agents miss out on golden opportunities to convert quality online leads. Corcoran says that if an agent can follow his ten principles of online lead conversion properly, his or her production could double within one year.

TIP 1: YOU HAVE TO CALL IMMEDIATELY

We live in an instant-gratification society. When a person inquires about a property listing, how long do you think he or she wants to wait to get the information? Not long, which is why speed is critical. Corcoran says, "The speed of the boss is the speed of the team," meaning that unless the person in charge of responding to online leads contacts the person, the operation will not move forward. This couldn't be truer, according to Corcoran, and the statistics don't lie. He pointed out a few key numbers.

- 95 percent of leads were successfully contacted when called within five minutes.
- 80 percent of leads were successfully contacted when called within ten to fifteen minutes. (Do you see how much a five minute difference can make?)
- After forty-five minutes, the contact percentage drops dramatically.

Another key statistic is that 68 percent of online leads will work with the first agent who responds to their request. This is another reason why calling leads immediately is critical.

TIP 2: E-MAIL EFFECTIVELY

According to Corcoran, the average person receives 147 e-mails per day. This much noise can consume a significant portion of a person's time. Although 71 of these 147 e-mails are deleted within five minutes and regarded as junk or spam, the average person spends two and a half hours reading, writing, and responding to the other e-mails each day. That equals almost thirteen hours of a person's time in a five-day workweek. Is this you? Most agents don't realize how much time they spend on e-mail because most e-mails aren't important. But these unimportant ones add up, absorbing time that could be used for prospecting and selling. Corcoran offered advice on how to build a better and more effective e-mail strategy.

- **Good:** Send a quick question via e-mail.
- **Better:** Send a quick question and a short message.
- **Best:** Include a compelling subject line (this gets them to open the e-mail, which is half the battle), a quick question for the prospect, and a short message.

TIP 3: USE VIDEO

Video is a powerful way to get your message across to people, yet few agents are actually using this highly effective medium. Corcoran recommended that agents regularly post videos on their social channels. People are much more likely to stop their news feed to watch a video than to read a post. People also remember photos and videos better than posts. Corcoran said that agents should even take their videos a step further by creating a blog or YouTube channel to host their video messages and client testimonials. This is also a great place for agents to highlight their communities and share videos from their most passionate fans.

TIP 4: CALL BACK FREQUENTLY

On his *Secrets* episode, Corcoran said he was amazed by how few agents actually follow up with online leads. He said that 48 percent of real estate professionals never follow up after the first call. Instead, they leave a voicemail and wait for the buyer or seller to call back, which often never happens. Corcoran said that one voicemail is not enough; to be most successful, agents must follow up with multiple calls. He then revealed other statistics regarding REALTORS® and online lead follow-up:

- One-quarter (25 percent) of agents make only two calls and then stop contacting the lead.
- Another 12 percent make three calls before stopping.
- Only 10 percent make more than three calls.
- A whole 5 percent never even call the online lead.

Corcoran said that although it may take several attempts to make the first contact with a lead, it usually takes several contacts to close it. Just how many, you ask? Corcoran drilled down on the numbers regarding how many contacts it took to close buyers.

When buyers buy (based on number of contacts with their agents):

- 2 percent buy on the first contact with an agent.
- 3 percent buy on the second contact.
- 5 percent buy on the third contact.

- 10 percent buy on the fourth contact.
- 80 percent buy after the fifth contact with an agent (the high was twelve contacts).

TIP 5: MASTER YOUR TIME

According to Corcoran, one of the biggest problems agents have is that they don't manage their time well. After saying this, Corcoran shared the following quote by Brandon Trean: "If you don't master your time, it is of a much higher probability that you will become an unconscious slave to people who have mastered theirs." He said that if agents could learn to master their time, they could live their dreams. He then showed the audience a system that can help REALTORS® better manage their time.

Step 1: Identify your "big rocks." Write out a list of everything that is important to you. Included in this should be family time, prospecting, meeting with your team to discuss KPIs (Key Performance Indicators), and anything else you enjoy doing or must do. (He refers to them as "rocks" because speakers often illustrate this point by showing an audience that a lot of rocks of different sizes can fit into a container only if you place the larger rocks into the container first and then add the smaller rocks.)

Step 2: Prioritize ruthlessly. After listing your "big rocks," it is time to organize them in order of importance. How much time do you want to spend on each big rock? How much time will these priorities require each day?

Step 3: Maximize your environment. You have heard the saying "Out of sight, out of mind," but how many times have you heard "In sight, in mind?" The key to maximizing your environment is staying focused on what needs to be done. Corcoran said that we spend an average of one and a half hours per day being distracted or looking for something. That adds up to seven and a half hours per week—almost an entire day of work. If you can stay focused on your time and manage the environment around you, you will be able to keep your big rocks "In sight, in mind."

An example of maximizing your environment is leveraging your listing presentations. Corcoran said many agents tell him they have a hard time getting buyers to sign Exclusive Buyer Agreement contracts. Corcoran said an easy solution to this problem is to have your sellers sign the Exclusive Buyer Agreement at the same time they sign their Exclusive Seller Agreement. Because most sellers will also be buyers, this is a perfect opportunity to maximize your environment and get both contracts signed at the same time.

Step 4: End of day routine. The most successful agents ask themselves four things at the end of the day. Doing this ensures that they have completed all their tasks and planned their activities for tomorrow. Here are the four questions that Corcoran said agents must ask themselves at the end of each day:

1. Did I call everyone I needed to call?
2. Did I e-mail everyone I needed to e-mail?
3. Did I promise to mail or send anything today?
4. What is my plan for tomorrow?

Corcoran had a coaching client go from sixty to more than four hundred leads in one month by asking these questions every day. Corcoran said he spends a lot of time with agents discussing how to maximize their environments for one reason: to help them focus on what is important in their lives and in their businesses. Time is a precious commodity, which is why Corcoran puts so much emphasis on scheduling. REALTORS® get paid to list, sell, prospect, and negotiate. It is important to sched-ule specific times for each of these activities. Below is an example of a schedule that Corcoran showed on his *Secrets* webinar. Scheduling and time blocking are critical to an agent's success; having a written schedule helps maximize daily productivity.

	Monday	Tuesday	Wednesday	Thursday	Friday	Sat-Sun
8:00 a.m.						
8:30 a.m.	Office Work	Office Work	Office Work	Office Work	Office Work	
9:00 a.m.	Calls/follow-up	Calls/follow-up	Calls/follow-up	Calls/follow-up	Calls/follow-up	
9:30 a.m.	Meeting	Prospecting	Prospecting	Prospecting	Prospecting	
10:00 a.m.	Meeting	Prospecting	Prospecting	Prospecting	Prospecting	
10:30 a.m.	Office Work	Office Work	Office Work	Office Work	Office Work	
11:00 a.m.	Appointment	Appointment	Appointment	Appointment	Appointment	
11:30 a.m.	Appointment	Appointment	Appointment	Appointment	Appointment	
12:00 p.m.	Lunch	Lunch	Lunch	Lunch	Lunch	
12:30 p.m.	Lunch	Lunch	Lunch	Lunch	Lunch	
1:00 p.m.	Office Work	Office Work	Office Work	Office Work	Office Work	
1:30 p.m.	Office Work	Office Work	Office Work	Office Work	Office Work	
2:00 p.m.	Calls/follow-up	Calls/follow-up	Calls/follow-up	Calls/follow-up	Calls/follow-up	
2:30 p.m.	Calls/follow-up	Calls/follow-up	Calls/follow-up	Calls/follow-up	Calls/follow-up	
3:00 p.m.	Appointment	Appointment	Appointment	Appointment	Appointment	
3:30 p.m.	Appointment	Appointment	Appointment	Appointment	Appointment	
4:00 p.m.	Appointment	Appointment	Appointment	Appointment	Appointment	
4:30 p.m.	Appointment	Appointment	Appointment	Appointment	Appointment	
5:00 p.m.	Office Work	Office Work	Office Work	Office Work	Office Work	
5:30 p.m.	Calls/follow-up	Calls/follow-up	Calls/follow-up	Calls/follow-up	Calls/follow-up	

Figure 11.1

Notice that appointments after 5:00 p.m. are visibly absent from the schedule. Corcoran said that this is mastering your time.

Most agents work around their clients' schedules without asking their clients to work around theirs. According to Corcoran, "One of the biggest mistakes an agent can make is to ask a client, 'When would you like to get together to look at homes?' The minute you do this, you throw your schedule out the window." Instead, he recommended asking, "What works better for you, mornings or afternoons?" Family time, date nights, and personal time are just as important, if not more important, than work. Do not neglect your personal or family time. "Plan your work, and work your plan."

TIP 6: PLAN YOUR CALLS

Corcoran Consulting conducted a study on when most phone leads come in. The study encompassed more than 460,000 inbound lead calls in a single year. What it found was that phone leads came in every single day of the week, with 34 percent of them coming in on Saturday and Sunday. It also found that about 50 percent of daily phone leads came in between the hours of 12:00 p.m. and 5:00 p.m. So what can agents take away from this study? First, have someone returning phone leads on the weekends, because Saturday and Sunday comprise more than one-third of all phone leads. Corcoran said that if you have a team, you should take the weekends off. Train your assistant to convert phone and online leads so you do not have to do it yourself on the weekends. This is a great opportunity for him or her to make money from your leads, so he or she should be excited about it. This is how you can maximize your call times. With regard to online leads, Corcoran found that they were more consistent throughout the week.

TIP 7: PROSPECT WITH INTENT

Not all leads are equal. Corcoran developed a lead prioritization strategy so agents can focus on the leads that generate the most money.

Corcoran said to sort your leads by price point and then call the highest-priced leads first. Not only will the commission be higher, but there is also a high probability that they have a house to sell as well. This strategy can give the agent the opportunity to get two commissions from the same client.

"Referral leads need to be called next," Corcoran said. These are leads from clients who gave a glowing review about you. They will already be strongly considering working with you. Make sure to mention the friend, associate, or family member who referred you to them. This will help strengthen the rapport with your new lead.

Next you should call leads who want to move in thirty days or less. Chances are they have a reason to move quickly, such as relocation for a new job. Corcoran also said to give the same level of priority to all leads who indicate they will be selling soon.

Finally, you should contact all other leads. These include people who do not currently own property, such as first-time home buyers and leads who are looking to buy in the next few months. Although all leads must be called, it is important to prioritize them. Prioritizing your leads will give you a higher probability of closing and will earn you higher-paying commissions.

TIP 8: HAVE A LEAD-MANAGEMENT SYSTEM

In addition to prioritizing your leads, having a CRM (Customer Relationship Management) or lead-management system is a must. Without one, agents will not be able to scale their businesses to the highest level because they will not be able to keep track of the conversations and notes from each client, especially as their databases grow. Corcoran said an easier way to organize your leads in a lead-management system is to classify your leads into categories.

"A" Leads. "A" leads are leads who are looking to buy or sell within the next thirty days. "With these leads, you should always have an appointment," Corcoran said. "You can't sell a house without an appointment." If you have a buyer or seller who is ready, willing, and able to buy right now, getting the appointment with that person is a must.

"B" Leads. These leads are people looking to buy within the next thirty to ninety days. They are very close to beginning their search, so it is important to make frequent contact with them. Corcoran recommended calling these leads twice per month, in weeks one and three, to check in with them and see if they are ready to begin their search. These leads should also be in an automated drip marketing campaign to increase the frequency of your contact with them.

"C" Leads. "C" leads are looking to buy or sell beyond ninety days. These leads need to be called once per month, during week two. They should be added to a drip marketing campaign as well.

Sphere of Influence. Your sphere of influence is your pipeline for referrals. These people need to be called once per month, in week four. They should also be put into a referral-type drip marketing campaign so you remain connected to them.

INFORMATION FORMS

Corcoran said that every lead you meet with should complete a buyer or seller form. These forms accomplish a few things:

1. They can help determine the level of motivation of the buyer or seller.
2. They can make it easier for them to focus on the particulars of their search (bedrooms, bathrooms, price, etc.).
3. They are consistent and ask the same questions, which makes it easier for you to enter the information into your CRM.

Here is an example from Corcoran's *Secrets* episode of a Buyer Information Sheet. You can view an example of a Seller Information Sheet in the webinar.

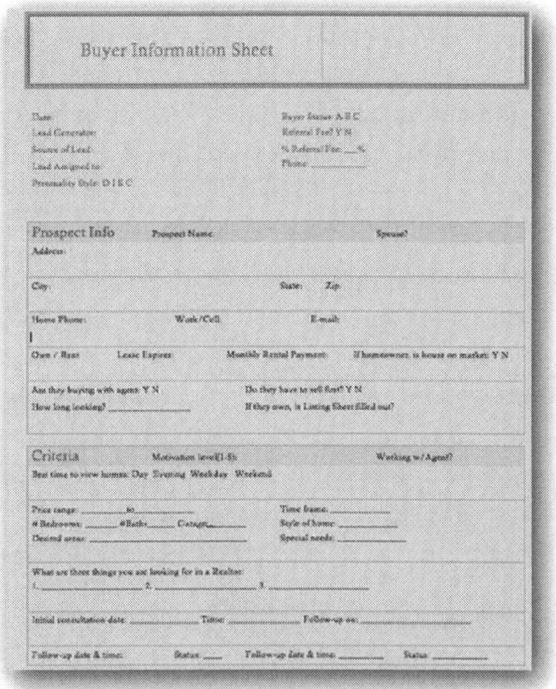
Buyer Information Sheet

Date:
Lead Generator:
Source of Lead:
Lead Assigned to:
Personality Style: D I S C

Buyer Status: A B C
Referral Fee? Y N
% Referral Fee: ___%
Phone: ________

Prospect Info — Prospect Name: — Spouse?
Address:
City: — State: — Zip:
Home Phone: — Work/Cell: — E-mail:
Own / Rent — Lease Expires: — Monthly Rental Payment: — If homeowner, is house on market: Y N
Are they buying with agent: Y N — Do they have to sell first? Y N
How long looking? ________ — If they own, is Listing Sheet filled out?

Criteria — Motivation level(1-5): — Working w/Agent?
Best time to view homes: Day Evening Weekday Weekend
Price range: ________ to ________ — Time frame: ________
Bedrooms: ______ #Baths ______ Garage ______ — Style of home: ________
Desired areas: ________ — Special needs: ________
What are three things you are looking for in a Realtor:
1. ________ 2. ________ 3. ________
Initial consultation date: ________ Time: ________ Follow-up on: ________
Follow-up date & time: — Status: ____ — Follow-up date & time: ________ — Status: ________

Figure 11.2 Sample Buyer Lead Form

TIP 9: KNOW YOUR NUMBERS

"The only way you can accomplish your goals and continue to grow and improve every year is to know your numbers," Corcoran said. Agents must set goals, and these goals should be focused on improvement from the previous year's sales. Corcoran recommended using three years of sales data derived from closed MLS sales. Once you have done this, break the closed sales down to the month in which the closings happen. Use this data to set your goals for the current or following year. The reason Corcoran recommended drilling down the data by month is because, due to seasonality, not all months will be equal. For example, an agent in Chicago might expect more sales in the summer months, while an agent in Miami may close more sales in the winter. The following page shows an example of how to set attainable goals for sales on a month-by-month basis, according to Corcoran's method.

Example - Sally Smith
To obtain your sales goal of fifty, stretch goal of sixty, and dream goal of seventy-five transactions this year, you will need to close the following sides each month.

	Goal	Actual	Stretch	Dream
January	3	3	3	4
February	3	4	4	5
March	4	5	5	6
April	5	5	6	7
May	5	7	6	7
June	5	5	6	7
July	5	5	5	7
August	4	6	5	7
September	4	4	4	6
October	5	5	5	7
November	4	5	5	6
December	3	6	6	6
Total/Year	50	60	60	75

Figure 11.3

CHECK OUT THESE NUMBERS

Corcoran Coaching and Consulting is big on data and statistics. They track every detail when it comes to agent phone calls, appointments, and closings, then break them down to dollars per hour. The students using Corcoran's system averaged the following at the time of his *Secrets* webinar, based on six million minutes of phone data:

- $2,191 per hour prospecting
- 40.93 dials per sale
- 1.61 appointments per sale

The most successful agents are experts in their markets. In addition to knowing about the housing prices, schools, and neighborhoods, agents must know how to leverage this knowledge when conversing with buyer or seller leads. For example, one of the first questions an agent usually asks when speaking with a buyer is, "Are you currently working with an agent?" Corcoran said that people would often answer yes just to get the agent to stay away. He offered a better strategy for asking this same question, one that is sure to have a much different effect on lead conversion.

The first question an agent should ask is, "How long have you been looking for a new home?" This accomplishes two things:

1. It tells you how long they have been active in the home-buying process.
2. It can help you determine if they are working with an agent.

If they do not indicate they are committed to an agent, Corcoran said to follow up with, "How many houses have you seen the inside of?" This may help differentiate whether they have been viewing their homes online or with an agent. If you still do not get a clear-cut answer, Corcoran said to follow up with, "How have you been viewing these homes?" This should give you the answer. However, just because they may have been viewing the homes through a different REALTOR® doesn't necessarily mean they are committed to him or her.

If they say they have been calling numbers on yard signs or connecting online with the listing agent for each property, they are not committed yet. Corcoran recommended saying, "Oh, so you've been calling the agent who represents the seller's best interests?" This is sure to get the buyers thinking about the importance of having an agent who represents *their* best interests.

TIP 10: KNOW YOUR CLIENT

Today we have a multitude of ways to communicate with one another. What might be the preferred method of communication for one person might be totally off limits for another. Corcoran said it is important to know your client's preferred method of communication. For example, traditionalists (people older than sixty-five) might be more comfortable with face-to-face conversation since this was the common method of real estate negotiation in the 1960s and 1970s. Baby boomers, those who are fifty to sixty-five in 2017, may prefer a phone call. A person from Generation X may prefer e-mail, while someone in Gen Y may prefer text messaging or social media. The most important thing to do is to ask your client or prospect what his or her preferred method of communication is. This will ensure a quicker response and help establish a stronger rapport.

FINAL THOUGHTS FROM BOB CORCORAN

Corcoran said that if agents can follow the ten tips he discussed in the webinar, they are guaranteed to be successful. The key to success is not just knowing about the principles, but living them every day. Without consistent reinforcement of these principles, many agents will eventually fail to have the breakthrough Corcoran discussed. This is why REALTORS® who are serious about taking their business to the next level (and staying there!) should consider employing a real estate coach or consultant.

Corcoran Coaching & Consulting offers both one-on-one coaching and corporate programs to help your business grow and succeed. Visit CorcoranCoaching.com or contact Corcoran directly at Bob@CorcoranCoaching.com to begin your journey to success.

Twelve

Austin Allison and Chris Smith

@GAustinAllison   @Chris_Smth

Peoplework

Austin Allison and Chris Smith are two of the biggest "young guns" in the real estate industry today. Both have massive followings on social media and are big draws on the speaking circuit. What they have been able to do in their respective businesses is merge design and fluidity into the way real estate transactions are done today. They were guests on *Secrets of Top Selling Agents* in late 2013 to discuss their book, the concept of Peoplework, and how it is changing the real estate industry.

Former *Secrets* guest Jimmy Mackin helped greatly in getting Allison and Smith to speak on our webinar series; he was the one who suggested them to Deb. For us, it was a no-brainer. Deb connected with the pair to schedule the event, which included one of the first looks into *Peoplework*—a book that has since sold more than fifteen thousand copies. This is a staggering figure considering that the book was self-published and was the first book either of them wrote. But when you can quote the likes of Helen Keller, JFK, and Jay-Z in the same book, you know it is going to be an interesting read.

Austin Allison is the founder and CEO of Dotloop, the premier transaction management network for the real estate industry. In 2012, he was named to the *Forbes* list of the "30 under 30." That same year, Inman News named him "Innovator of the Year." He has been included on the Inman "100 Most Influential People" list numerous times and was featured in a cover story for *Entrepreneur* magazine. More than 650,000 professionals are using Dotloop's services today, and in 2015, the Zillow Group acquired it for $108 million.

Chris Smith was the chief Peopleworker of Dotloop at the time of the book release. He and Allison would meet weekly to discuss how they could continually improve processes and person-to-person interaction. Smith also hosted the #WaterCooler webinar series and runs Curaytor with his cofounder, Jimmy Mackin.

HOW PEOPLEWORK CAME ABOUT

Peoplework is about putting people first in a digital world, according to Allison. As a young REALTOR®, he found himself spending a lot of time driving around and standing next to fax machines to send and receive documents. He couldn't believe how disconnected the industry was. There were very few people-to-people interactions in the transaction process. Faxes were flying back and forth, and documents had to be sent to multiple parties. This was a problem, and it was only getting worse. Allison wondered what happened to the days when things were face-to-face and belly-to-belly. Transactions could be much smoother if the parties could just work things out in person. There had to be a better way to do things, he thought. This experience was the vision behind Dotloop, the company he would later found. By combining person-to-person interactions with the power of today's technology, Dotloop became a disruptor to the real estate industry. As Smith put it in their *Secrets* webinar, "Technology accelerates greatness." Dotloop was soon born, as were the Peoplework principles they shared in their *Secrets* episode.

PRINCIPLE 1: P2P REPLACES B2B AND B2C

"Before the digital revolution, there were limited fractures in the communication chain," Allison said in *Peoplework*. Things like terms of sale and negotiated price were exchanged "belly to belly." The Digital Revolution caused a fracture in this dynamic, and communication and business interactions became choppy.

Those in Peoplework businesses need to think of their interactions as one person dealing with another (P2P), not just about the numbers. Allison and Smith brought up a great example on *Secrets* about why agents should view leads as P2P. Too many agents view leads as just another number. P2P agents view leads as people. They work to build lasting relationships—real business relationships that pay off in multiples.

Smith mentioned three companies that live and breathe the P2P model: eLance, a platform for freelancers worldwide to do contract work for people at the prices they set; Airbnb, the home- and room-sharing platform that is taking the hospitality industry by storm; and Task Rabbit, where people seeking to earn extra money run errands or tasks for customers for a fee. P2P principles have been a main driver behind the success of these companies.

PRINCIPLE 2: HUMAN COMPANIES WIN

If you can implement the principles from principle 1, you can succeed at principle 2. Most businesses care about their customers, but they still put the numbers first in their order of priorities. Doing this will take some of the humanity away from the business because the two components will eventually conflict with one another.

Peoplework companies, on the other hand, put people first. They think about customers as family, and family is the best model for lifetime retention. Because the entire digital "grid" is made up of people, it is the human companies that will win. The formula is quite basic: **enhancing the human element = customer loyalty**. It is that simple.

Smith brought up a personal story about this principle. He was in an airport and was running late for his flight. When he finally got to the gate, the gate was closed, and the attendant refused to reopen it for him. But what if the gate attendant had been a close friend or relative? Do you think she may have gone the extra mile and asked the captain to allow her friend on board? Probably. This is the power of Peoplework.

In the *Peoplework* book, Allison and Smith point to seven core pillars that make up a humanity-based company. Peoplework companies practice these concepts every day.

1. You must think about your business like a person who lives, breathes, and evolves. Apply your own personality.
2. You must be genuine and transparent.
3. You must establish genuine human principles and core values.
4. You must care, and show it, every chance you get.
5. You must invest in change and systems and continuously improve.
6. You must intertwine the principles and values that you embrace into every inch of your company's fabric.
7. You must manifest these principles with mission statements, a code of ethics, and an employee manual.

An example that Smith featured on *Secrets* was Tom's Shoes. Tom's Shoes donates a pair of shoes to needy children around the world for every pair the company sells. Why do they do this? Because Tom's Shoes is a company that has taken humanity as a business principle to the next level.

PRINCIPLE 3: CHANGE REQUIRES A BLUEPRINT

Change is the new normal. In *Peoplework*, Allison and Smith said that change is not a *yes or no* question; it's a *yes and how* question. The question is, "How are you going to change?" The pair offered some solid advice, suggesting books, leadership conferences, blogs, search engines, and social media as good places to start. "In a people revolution, businesses must continue to learn their craft," Allison said. "They need to keep their axes sharp."

Change actually happens on two fronts: the internal one with one's self, and the external one with clients/customers. Typically, the more established someone is in his or her career, the more he or she will have to work to change. Internally, one should monitor how he or she is implementing change. Externally, agents can crowd-source feedback from clients on social media or by sending customer surveys in e-mail.

When Marissa Mayer took over the reins at Yahoo, much change was needed. She began buying companies and then quickly shutting them down. Why did she do this? She did it because she wasn't interested in the companies themselves. She was interested only in the talented people behind the companies. The people were extremely valuable and would be integral to influencing change at Yahoo.

Smith also discussed the failed change attempt that former Apple VP Ron Johnson implemented during his brief tenure with JCPenny. Johnson had worked wonders in the retail and design of Apple stores, and he assumed he could replicate his success at JCPenny's. The result was an epic failure that alienated many of JCPenny's core customers. Why did Johnson fail so miserably? He made the classic mistake of assuming that what worked at one company would automatically work at another. Apple and JCPenney are polar opposites in retail, and Johnson didn't get to know the customer base and what they wanted from their stores. For change to be successful, you must understand your customer.

PRINCIPLE 4: PURPOSE BEFORE TECHNOLOGY

In his *Secrets of Top Selling Agents* episode, Allison said that companies often make the mistake of putting features and functions before people. The key is to put purpose before technology. Purpose provides focus, which can help an agent zero in on technology that really matters.

Austin Allison used Dotloop as an example of a company putting purpose before technology. When REALTORS® call Dotloop to sign up, the most common reason they give for why they are signing up is that they wish to go paperless. "But going paperless is merely a by-product," Allison said. "The real purpose is to make the transaction easier. What agents really want is to run a better and more efficient business, as well as to create a better experience for their clients."

Business leaders often think technology solves problems, but it doesn't, according to Allison and Smith. Technology should be a part of the solution, for sure, but you cannot start there. First, there has to be a purpose.

Allison and Smith used the Nest learning thermostat as an example. Nest is a great, user-friendly piece of technology that allows homeowners to program and control their heat and air conditioning from their phones. But it would never have gotten off the ground if it weren't built around a purpose. The purpose was to save consumers money by optimizing their energy usage with an easy-to-use device. The technology followed the purpose, and Nest was a smash success that Google eventually purchased for $3 billion.

PRINCIPLE 5: QUALITY CREATES QUANTITY

If REALTORS® (and businesses) focused on quality rather than quantity, their businesses would grow at a better pace, according to Allison. Too many agents put their focus on the top of the funnel (e.g., leads) rather than focusing on nurturing the leads they have. Peoplework turns this model upside down.

In the Peoplework method, quality products and services enhance the consumer experience and create loyalty and referrals. Allison and Smith stressed that less is actually more in Peoplework. Focus on fewer leads and deliver amazing experiences every time. A few customers will become many more over time. Smith discussed Starbucks as an example of a company living this principle. Starbucks doesn't view a customer as one transaction, but rather as a lifetime of value. By nurturing the business of each individual customer, Starbucks creates many more opportunities to make money. The average Starbucks customer visits the store four times per week and spends an average of five dollars per visit. How is that for lifetime value and repeat business?

The main differentiator between you and your competition is how you interact with your clients. Focus on quality, not quantity. Allison and Smith offered three steps to help people create more quality in their work. They cover these steps in more detail in *Peoplework*:

Step 1: Figure out who you want to be.
Step 2: Define the experience you will provide with the end user in mind.
Step 3: Deliver on the promise.

PRINCIPLE 6: SERVICE IS MARKETING

This principle is built off principle 5. Allison said on *Secrets* that traditionally, service was thought of as overhead. It was a cost of doing business—an afterthought. For Peoplework customers, however, service is more than an overhead cost—it is marketing. When a company provides superior service, customers tell their friends. Word-of-mouth marketing is the most powerful kind of marketing.

Zappos is a great example of a company that has been built on customer service. Relationship marketing was the business model from day one, which developed into customer loyalty and repeat business. This helped the company grow into one of the leading online shoe stores in the world.

Peoplework offers a step-by-step process for how to develop a superior customer service system. It starts with defining your or your company's vision and expectations. Once these are established, three rules must be followed:

1. Be available by giving the consumer options (online/phone/chat).
2. Deliver value, and don't expect anything in return.
   a. Answer customer questions without expecting something in return.
   b. Answers should be functional, relevant, and appropriate.
3. Delivering great service will bring great reward.

PRINCIPLE 7: BUSINESSES ARE BUILT ON COMMUNITIES

Thanks to digital innovation, the world is more connected than ever. Although this innovation may make it seem easier than ever to acquire clients, there has been a real disconnect in people-to-people interaction, according to Allison. The most successful businesses overcome this noise and stay connected by building communities. Communities are real and scalable while maintaining a level of people-to-people intimacy.

In today's world, communities are bigger than ever, thanks to the power of social media. As a business, you have to be actively conscious about building your own community. Smith and Allison brought up Apple as an example of a passionate community of loyalists. It didn't happen by accident. Apple sells great products and makes a lot of money, but the company also pro-vides its community with valuable information and help that they don't charge for. They genuinely care about the customers in their community. Don't know what to build a community about? According to Allison and Smith, niche markets can be great for building communities.

CREATING YOUR COMMUNITY

According to *Peoplework*, there are four tribal rules to follow when building your community:

1. Exist for a greater purpose, not just to sell.
    a. Tribal businesses exist to solve bigger problems.
    b. Communities are built around passion and purpose.
2. Content marketing builds tribes.
    a. Change requires a blueprint.
    b. Leverage social media and your community together.

3. Stop selling immediately.
   a. Define the greater purpose, and exist for it.
4. Do less talking and more facilitating.

Allison and Smith have both built communities around their companies. They have a loyal following with passionate members. They live this principle every day in their businesses.

PRINCIPLE 8: PASSION POWERS PROFIT

People who follow traditional business practices misunderstand passion. They mistake professionalism, efficiency, and profits for passion. Although these principles may please investors and shareholders, is it sustainable in the long run if it is just about the money? Probably not. In today's people-first era, it is passion that powers the most profit (think of Apple). "You do better work with more conviction when you're passionate about something," Allison said.

Allison gave a great real estate example of passion and focus on *Secrets of Top Selling Agents*. A woman told him that she was really passionate about working with buyers and wanted that to be her primary focus. He then asked her what she would do if someone wanted her to list a $2 million home. The answer is that she should refer it to a listing agent. Although many agents think that it would be crazy to do this, in theory taking the listing goes against her passion and expertise. Would she be doing the sellers justice if she just listed the property and earned a big paycheck, even if her heart wasn't in it?

"The secret to getting the most out of both life and business is to figure out what you are passionate about and then spend as much time as possible on it," Smith said. He then brought up Mark Zuckerberg of Facebook as an example. Yahoo offered Zuckerberg $2 billion for his company when he was only twenty-three years old. He turned them down. People thought he was crazy. Why would he do this? He did it because his passion for Facebook and connecting the world was more important than money.

The key to discovering your passion is asking yourself if you are happy with your life and how you are spending your time. If you can answer this question with a yes, then you can have clarity about what you really want to pursue.

PRINCIPLE 9: STARS ARE MADE IN HOLLYWOOD

Is it coincidence that many of the biggest movie stars, directors, writers, and studio executives live within a twenty-mile radius of Hollywood? The answer is no. Hollywood is the epicenter of the film industry. If you are a burgeoning actor and want to get noticed, you have a much greater chance if you are living in Hollywood than if you are hundreds or thousands of miles away. This is the theme behind Peoplework principle 9.

On *Secrets*, Allison said that it is vital to surround yourself with an all-star team. You need the best people—people who are aligned with your passion and vision. Your success will be determined by whom you surround yourself with. In their book, Allison and Smith offer three key elements required for using passion to build your all-star team:

1. **Living proof.** Surround yourself with people who have "been there and done that." It cuts your learning curve exponentially and helps you reach the next level much faster.

2. **Access to the network.** Think about Hollywood. If you know many of the major players, you increase your chances of being noticed. Go where the talent is in your area, and start networking.

3. **Culture.** Build a culture that supports your vision. Get rid of the people who are bad for the culture.

Smith brought up one of his all-time favorite teams as an example on *Secrets*: The Chicago Bulls dynasty of the late 1990s. He said that although Michael Jordan was the best player on the planet, he could not have won his six NBA titles without a supporting cast and a great "director," Coach Phil Jackson. Jordan had Scottie Pippin, Dennis Rodman, and other specialists on his team, and together they became an unstoppable force.

PRINCIPLE 10: ONLY YOU WRITE THE STORY

The only person who can determine what you become or what difference you make in the world is you. It's a good-news, bad-news scenario, according to Allison. The bad news is that it is up to you to make it happen. The good news, however, is that there has never been a better time in history to do it. Allison mentioned Mark Zuckerberg and Steve Jobs on the webinar as two people who have had a massive impact on the world because of their passion and determination.

Allison concluded by quoting Steve Jobs about the difference between young people and old people: "Older people look at an object or problem and ask, 'What is it?' Younger people will look at the same object or problem and ask, 'What can I do with it?'" The message here is to be more like the younger person. Combining this type of curiosity with the proven Peoplework principles can take your business to a whole new level.

Looking for more great advice from Allison and Smith? Visit Amazon.com and purchase your copy of *Peoplework* for more tips on running a people-first business in a digital world.

Thirteen

Leigh Brown

@LeighBrown

Real and Powerful Buyer/Seller Scripts and Dialogues for Today's Market

Leigh Brown not only talks the talk; she walks the walk. A power agent in the Greater Charlotte area, Brown has a record that speaks for itself. She is a member of RE/MAX's Circle of Legends and has achieved Diamond status for sales. In addition to her stellar career as a REALTOR®, Brown is an accomplished speaker who shows agents how they can grow their businesses and adapt to any market. Her speaking has taken her to such events as the Alaska Association of REALTORS® and the REIQ Summit in Queensland, Australia. She is also a speaker for NAR, CRS, and RPAC. In May 2012, she was our guest on *Secrets of Top Selling Agents*, where she showed agents how to use the power of scripts to connect with consumers.

When Deb Helleren contacted Brown and asked her if she would be interested in being a guest on *Secrets*, Brown jumped at the chance. I was excited about sharing the stage with her. Previously, I had met Brown only in passing. However, I was well aware of her reputation as a top-producing and very approachable agent. Her episode was unique in the sense that no one has done one quite like it before or since. It was timeless and can be tweaked to use in any market.

WHY SCRIPTS?

When Brown talks about "scripts," she doesn't mean people should read a script when talking to a client or prospect. That would be awkward. You are likely to sound "canned" unless you practice. Failing to practice a script or dialogue would be like an athlete showing up on game day without ever having practiced.

"Scripts are nothing more than a starting point," Brown said on *Secrets*. They are there to help you respond when the same situations keep presenting themselves. If you botch a prospecting call because you did not have a response to a certain question, you want to make sure that you are ready for it the next time someone asks it. The best way to prepare is to develop a script or response and then practice so that when the time comes, it rolls off your tongue instinctively. Practice makes perfect, and Brown said it is not just the words you use but your body language as well. Body language can tell a lot about a person and his or her confidence level. You must rehearse both verbal and body language.

To validate Brown's point, Deb Helleren and Mel McMurrin polled the audience during her *Secrets* episode to find out how many agents on the webinar used scripts. The results were convincing: Of those polled, 29 percent said they use scripts all the time, 29 percent said they never use scripts, and 42 percent said they use scripts some of the time.

Altogether, 71 percent of the REALTORS® on the webinar said they used scripts at least some of the time. Brown summed it up by saying, "If you find yourself saying the same thing over and over to prospects and clients, it's a script."

SOME IMPORTANT DO'S AND DON'TS

Before discussing scripts, Brown mentioned some important things to be aware of that can make a big difference in your business.

1. **Do avoid industry jargon.** Make sure people understand what you are trying to tell them. Do not use acronyms like CMA and REO without first asking clients if they understand what these terms mean.
2. **Don't ask for referrals; ask for recommendations.** Brown said it not only sounds better, but has also made a difference in her business. Be sure to use the recommender's name in your follow-up.
3. **Do realize that online reviews are huge today.** Review sites like Yelp, Google Reviews, and Facebook

offer consumers the opportunity to rate and review REALTORS® and other businesses. Be proactive; ask your happy clients to leave a review about you on one of these sites.

"HOW'S THE MARKET?"

Perhaps the most asked question for any REALTOR® is "How's the market?" Brown said to be prepared for this question, because it can often lead to a great referral or sale opportunity. Most people do not want to be bored with statistics (although some do). Brown said she preferred something catchy like, "The market is moving; do you know someone who needs to move?" Another script she discussed on the webinar is, "Real estate is an adventure every day. Do you know someone who needs me?" Both responses answer the question, which is good, and also follow up with a question. If the person wants specifics, it could be because he or she is considering buying or selling. Agents often miss a huge opportunity for business because they fail to ask. This question could be a signal that someone is getting ready to make a move. Always be prepared to answer and follow up to it.

RENTALS

If a person asks you how the rental market is, what would you say? Many agents assume that the person is merely looking to rent. "Not so," Brown said. A good question to start with is, "Are you looking to become a landlord?" The person may actually be looking for investment property, which could be a huge opportunity for you. If he or she says no, Brown then recommended asking, "Do you know someone who needs to rent?" This will get to the bottom of why the person asked the question. Again, never make assumptions. You could miss out on representing an investment buyer.

HOME STAGING

When taking a listing, it is important to rate it on a scale of one to ten, with ten being a perfect home in spotless condition with the latest updates, and one being a home in nasty condition with pee on the carpet and broken windows. Brown has found that the homes that sell the fastest in most markets are the nines and tens, followed by the ones and twos (mostly for teardown or rehab purposes). However, most homes for sale are situated somewhere in the middle, typically between six and eight. Home staging is the perfect way to take a home that is a seven or eight and elevate it to a nine or ten. Whether the home is vacant or being lived in by homeowners, it is important to stage it for every showing, and it is the agent's responsibility to reinforce the importance of this step. Home staging can mean the difference between a quick sale at top dollar and a long market time culminating in a discounted sale.

OVERCOMING OBJECTIONS

For the following objections, it does not matter what type of market you are in. Your clients in both hot and cold markets will use them. Brown suggested the following answers to these common objections.

Seller objection: "Let's try a higher price."

On *Secrets*, Brown said she likes to use a grocery-store analogy when responding to this objection. After reviewing the CMA and comparable properties with her client, Brown will ask, "Do you want to be on the top shelf where few people see you, or do you want to be at eye level for maximum exposure?"

Seller objection: "We can always come down in price later. What's the big deal?"

Brown responds to this objection by explaining the importance of coming out of the gate at the right price, and then she goes back to her food comparison. "If you put bananas on the top shelf, by the time you move them down to eye level, they are overripe, and the only way they will sell is at a discount." This is what usually happens to listings with long market times.

Seller objection: "Will you reduce your commission?"

Brown said she makes her answer to this question simple: "Just say no and move on." The problems usually begin when agents stumble while trying to explain their value to clients. Trying to do this can backfire on you. If the sellers keep pressing about reducing the commission, Brown recommended responding by posing the question to them: "This is my job. This is how I get paid. If your boss asks you for a thirty percent reduction in salary so your company can make its numbers, would you do it?" They can relate to this.

Seller objection: "I'm not doing repairs."

Brown challenges her sellers to consider the repair process. At the time of the listing, she explains to them the home-inspection process, a process she calls the "extortion period" because during the process buyers can make repair demands or ask for a credit, threatening to walk away from the deal unless their requests are satisfied. Buyers often use the home inspection as an additional negotiation, and Brown prepares her sellers for this. After explaining the "extortion period," she will prepare a net sheet for the seller and include a dollar amount for repairs in it. This way, the sellers are prepared in case an issue comes up at the inspection. If the sellers object, she simply reminds them that normal wear and tear on a home ranges between $100 and $1,000 for every year they have lived in the home, depending on the size and condition of the property. Often, the demands total a credit request of $500 to $1,000.

If the seller balks at the request, this is Brown's response: "You've just sold your house for X dollars. All the buyers want is a six-hundred-dollar credit and the deal will move forward. Do you really want to buy back the house from them for six hundred dollars? Are you really willing to lose the deal over six hundred dollars?" It is often a matter of pride for the sellers, not money. Brown said that if you can get this point across to your sellers, they will often see the wisdom in giving the credit to the buyer.

Seller objection: "Showings aren't convenient."
According to Brown, this objection is pretty easy to overcome. She simply says, "Buyers can't buy the house if they can't see it. The more difficult you make it for buyers to see the house, the less likely they are to buy it." Buyers make a lot of assumptions when they cannot see the home.

Brown also does her best to remove emotion from the transaction by telling sellers that they are "liquidating an asset" instead of "selling a house." This has proven to make transactions go much smoother for Brown and her team.

Buyer objection: "Can you meet me at night? Or on Sunday morning?"

Brown said she doesn't work on evenings or Sundays. She does not let buyers dictate her schedule. Instead, she gives them time slots she has available and rarely has a problem with this. "The biggest mistake agents make," Brown said, "is that they revolve their schedule around clients, not the other way around." Agents are not punching bags. They are professionals. They are entitled to have lives. And having a life as a real estate agent is possible, especially if they give the available options to the buyers. Consumers would rather wait in line for quality than work with a desperate agent.

When Brown is asked if she can show homes at night, she simply says, "No, but I am available between eighty-thirty in the morning and four-thirty in the afternoon." If someone asks her to show homes on a weekend, she says, "Weekends are reserved for out-of-town buyers. Perhaps you can meet me before you go to the office or on your lunch break? Or maybe you can skip lunch and get off early so we can see these houses?"

Another concern is REALTOR® safety. Agents have been assaulted and harmed during showings because they met clients they didn't know at a vacant house for an evening showing. Brown said it is important to have your first meeting with new clients at the office. This gives you an opportunity to get to know them, and vice versa. Brown recommended asking for their driver's license and having them fill out a client information form. Although this may sound weird, it is not. Think about it. Consumers have to show an ID to fill out forms when opening a bank account or applying for a mortgage. Why should this be any different?

Buyer objection: Lowball offers

Novice buyers often think that making a lowball offer is perfectly normal. Although a low offer is sometimes justified, Brown cautioned buyers who want to make obscenely low offers that make no sense. She tells her buyers that not every seller will counter a low offer, especially if the sellers feel insulted by it. She often uses a restaurant analogy to handle this objection.

"If a waiter simply asks you if you want dessert, it is easy to refuse. That is usually the end of the conversation. However, if the waiter asks the same question while he has a tray of delicious desserts in front of you, it is much more tempting. Make the offer more tempting, and you have a much better chance of getting the home at a good price."

After her presentation, Brown fielded questions from the webinar audience. Many questions were asked. I have chosen to present the two whose answers I felt were most beneficial for agents.

Q: What should you say if you don't have many (or any) listings, and a seller asks how many listings you have?

A: Brown said this is an easy question to answer. "At this time, I don't have many listings, which means that your listing will get one hundred percent of my attention." This statement can actually be backed up by a couple of studies, including one conducted by Longwood University and Central Florida University. This study found that REALTORS® with many listings (fifteen or more) do a worse job selling houses than REALTORS® with fewer. Listings held by agents with more than fifteen listings take an average of 26 percent longer to sell than those belonging to agents with fewer than fifteen. Do not feel uncomfortable answering this question. You have data on your side.

Q: "What if buyers want to work only with the listing agent?"
A: Brown said, "You need to have the agency conversation with the buyers right away." Many buyers feel that if they work with the listing agent, they will somehow get a better deal. It is not true. The problem is that most agents don't have this conversation with buyers. This lack of communication can cost them the deal. Brown said the best thing to say is, "I work one hundred percent with buyers or sellers, but not in a dual role. If I am in a dual role, how can I pledge my loyalty to both parties?" Buyers usually realize at this point that it is not a good idea to work with the listing agent.

Leigh Brown's webinar gave agents insight on how to prepare for and answer common questions and objections. It is this preparation that has made her one of America's top REALTORS®. But this success didn't happen by accident. Brown uses scripts and rehearses her presentations to ensure that she gets the listing or the deal done with the best possible terms for her clients. I recommend watching the episode in its entirety to get even more great information from her. You will be glad you did.

For even more great advice on successfully dealing with clients, visit NoFluffTraining.com to see if Leigh Brown will be speaking in a city near you. You can also visit OutrageousAuthenticity.com to purchase your copy of Brown's must-read book, *Outrageous Authenticity.*

Fourteen

Joe Sesso

@joesesso

It's Your Time to Shine

Now that you have learned the "secrets" of some of the most successful and powerful people in real estate, the question is, "What are *you* going to do with them?" Are you going develop a game plan based on what you have learned? Are you going to become a top-producing agent? Or are you going to let an incredible opportunity slip away? The choice is yours.

The people featured in this book come from all walks of life and are from different parts of the United States. Despite these differences, they are similar in many ways. They all have tremendous ambition and drive, and they are all innovative. From Barbara Corcoran's *Corcoran Report*, to Austin Allison's Dotloop, to Raj Qsar's video techniques, every person featured in this book has become a leader in the real estate industry through these qualities. Most of all, they never gave up, no matter how tough things got.

Imagine being a broker-owner of a profitable business one moment and the next moment having it cut in half. That's what happened to Barbara Corcoran. Did she give up and let her ex-boyfriend ruin her life? No, she was more determined than ever to not only succeed, but to prove that she could do so without him. After selling her business for $55 million, I think she proved her point—many times over!

Dave Liniger not only changed the way agents get compensated with the cofounding of RE/MAX, he changed the way franchising was done. He built RE/MAX into the largest real estate franchise in the world. After almost tragically losing his life, Liniger fought back with the power of positive thinking and a strong support group to not only survive his ordeal, but thrive. Will you give up when the going gets tough, or will you fight back the way Dave Liniger did?

Gary Keller accomplished more by the time he was thirty than most people do in an entire lifetime. Despite his massive success, he never slowed down. Since growing Keller Williams into a real estate powerhouse, Keller has dedicated himself to giving back and helping others. *The ONE Thing* is a guidebook for transforming all aspects of one's life, from health to family to business. If there is one book that can make you a better and more productive person, *The ONE Thing* is it.

Social media has become an integral part of marketing and self-promotion today for all industries. Nobody does a better job of teaching social-media best practices than Katie Lance. With so many social-media "gurus" out there, it's hard to stand out, but Lance has been able to consistently stand above the crowd because she works at being the best every single day. Social media is constantly evolving, and no one knows this more than Lance. She continues to find new and unique ways for people to use social media to get their messages across. Besides providing a wealth of knowledge on social media, REALTORS® should also understand the importance of constantly being aware of changes and innovations in their industry. Don't let it pass you by. Your clients will take notice.

Raj Qsar has taken technology to a whole new level with his amazing real estate videos. Although not every agent or company can afford to create some of the videos he produces, Qsar has proven that striving to be the best makes a difference. Customers actually seek his company out to list their properties because they want the same quality of video and marketing that their neighbor or friend got from the Boutique Real Estate Group. Are you the type of person who settles for being mediocre, or do you truly want to be the best?

I featured Chris Smith twice in this book for two reasons. First, the episodes were on completely different topics, and second, he is one of the most amazing influencers in the industry today. I'm also happy to call him my friend. I've known Chris Smith since we both worked for Move.com. He began as an outside sales rep for Top Producer. His job was to cold-call REALTORS® and set up in-office demonstrations. But Smith didn't want to be just an account executive. He was very determined to succeed and soon realized that agents really enjoyed listening to the information he was providing. His rise from account executive to chief evangelist at Inman News happened incredibly fast. Personally, I've never seen anyone rise this fast in the industry. But Smith's success is well deserved. He is truly an innovative and driven professional in every sense of the word. His story is another testament to why striving to go above and beyond what everyone else is doing works. People take notice and will seek you out, because they want to work with the best.

Not everyone can produce interesting, original content that people will absolutely love, but everyone can be useful. The problem is, most people refuse to be useful unless they are getting compensated for it. They want a *quid pro quo.* Jay Baer showed numerous examples of how businesses are winning customers over by being more useful to them. If you don't think of yourself as an innovator, try being more useful to your prospects. You would be surprised by how much you will stand out among your competitors. This is true innovation.

Real estate can be a very stressful business. It is easy to get behind on things like e-mail. No one wants to log into their e-mail account and see hundreds or even thousands of unopened e-mails. There is nothing more stressful than that. In chapter eight, Jimmy Mackin showed you how to better organize and prioritize your e-mails so you can eventually get to *inbox zero.* At first glance, this chapter might not seem like a secret that can help you make a lot of money. However, if you can promptly respond to e-mails and effectively use tools like Boomerang and Yesware (e-mail tracking), you can better identify opportunities to contact your clients when they are thinking about you or your materials. Don't neglect the cool technologies revealed in this chapter.

Think about Tom Ferry's quote in chapter nine: "The rich and the rest both hate to do what it takes to be successful, but the rich do it anyway." Everyone hates cold-calling, door knocking, and prospecting FSBOs and expired listings, but the most successful agents are the ones who keep doing it with smiles on their faces. They take rejection as just another "no" on the way to "yes." They see the light at the end of the tunnel, and they have a plan to get to the next level. Is that you?

One "secret" that stands out in this book is having a niche in real estate. Raj Qsar's niche is high-quality video. Barbara Corcoran's was Manhattan real estate. Kelly Mitchell discussed the importance of carving out a niche in your marketplace. If you are having trouble identifying a niche opportunity in your market, watch Mitchell's *Secrets of Top Selling Agents* episode to learn how to better identify unique and profitable niches in real estate. Don't be a jack-of-all-trades. If you want to stand out, you have to be different.

One of the most profitable areas of lead generation and conversion is online. Why are some agents really good at converting online leads while others are not? There is a science to converting online leads, and Bob Corcoran laid out a ten-step program to mastering it in chapter 11. If you invest in online leads from portals like Homes.com, you need to make sure that you have a system in place that maximizes lead conversion. If you have failed at online lead conversion in the past, it is probably because you didn't have a system in place. I encourage you to go back and watch Bob Corcoran's *Secrets* episode. It will give you a whole new perspective on how to attack online leads.

Austin Allison saw a fracture in the communication system of real estate transactions, and this spawned the idea for Dotloop. Even if you may not create a business that facilitates real estate transactions the way Allison did, remember that you are in a service business. Focus on better customer service, and don't neglect the power of face-to-face interaction. It will make a difference in your business, especially regarding referrals.

The best performers in the world spend a lot of time practicing. Whether it is an actor trying to memorize his or her lines for a movie or Michael Jordan being the last person to leave the gym because he wanted to work on his free throws, the best performers take nothing for granted. You shouldn't either. This is where scripts and dialogues come into play. Don't go into a listing presentation and just "wing it." Be prepared. That is how Leigh Brown got to be one of the top RE/MAX agents in the United States. Practice makes perfect, and you don't want to lose a $10,000 commission because you weren't prepared to answer a simple question.

As you can see, each *Secrets of Top Selling Agents* guest I have featured in this book revealed a different "secret" for agents to use in their businesses. The ingredients for success are on these pages. The very people who spoke about them on *Secrets of Top Selling Agents* have proven their effectiveness. Ultimate success won't be easy. If it were, everyone would be successful. It will take hard work, guts, innovation, and determination to be the best in your market. But there is no doubt that if you follow the systems that have been described on the *Secrets of Top Selling Agents* webinars and in this book, you can do it. No matter how hard things may get, always stay positive. Always remember the famous words of basketball coach Jim Valvano: "Don't give up. Don't ever give up."

You can find more great real estate business tips at Secrets-ofTopSellingAgents.com. Check out the fantastic recorded webinars or check back each month to catch the next live one, all at no cost! To schedule a speaking engagement at your office, visit JoeSesso.com.

About the Author

Joe Sesso is the national speaker and director of national sales for Homes.com. He has shown more than thirty thousand agents in forty-nine states how to maximize their real estate marketing and sales strategies using the power of technology and social media, drawing on proven case studies from some of the leading business schools in the United States. He has been with Homes.com since 2011. Prior to his tenure at Homes.com, Sesso was the national speaker for Realtor.com.

Joe has been a licensed real estate agent since 2000. From 2000 to 2003, he specialized in foreclosure investment and sales at Troy Realty in Chicago. From 2003 through 2008, Joe was part of an investment team that bought and sold more than $10 million in foreclosure real estate. That work became the inspiration for his first book, *The Foreclosure Revolution*. It won an Axiom Business Book award in 2009.

Joe has a bachelor's degree and an MBA from Indiana University and a master of global management degree from the Thunderbird School of Global Management at Arizona State University.

Made in the USA
Columbia, SC
09 November 2017

SEAN TULIEN

About the Author

Sean Tulien has been hooked on science fiction ever since the eighth grade, when he read a story about a man who got trapped in a teleportation device. Today, he still loves to read books, but now he writes and edits them, too. When he's not working with words, Sean can be found playing video games, listening to loud and abrasive music, or wearing himself out in the gym. Sean lives in Minnesota with his lovely and encouraging wife, Nicolle.

Questions to Think About

1. In this story, Liam is often a pessimist. He doesn't trust Litchfield and expects the worst of him. But Grace is more of an optimist. She believes Litchfield is working to do good. Who are you more like, Liam or Grace? Using examples from your own life, explain why you feel that you are either a pessimist or an optimist.

2. Liam and Grace live in a futuristic world, a world that has been devastated by nuclear meltdowns. But what do you think life will be like seventy years from now? Write a story about living in the future. What new problems might you face, and how will your daily life change?

3. Kerrigan's life goal is to correct a mistake he made that plunged the world into an energy crisis. Have you ever made a mistake that you felt you needed to fix? What did you do? How did it affect the people around you? And what did you do to correct things? Did everyone appreciate your efforts to fix your mistake?

DEEP WATER HOTEL

Michael suffers from a mysterious and painful lung disease. But he's thrilled when his favorite online celebrity raises the funds to grant his last wish—to visit the world's only deep-water hotel. Submerged miles below the water's surface, Michael discovers horrifying sea creatures, and a shocking secret is revealed.

THE FRIEND

Kat and Allie have been friends forever. But when Allie returns from a summer away, everything changes. Allie's different. Too different. And Kat begins to wonder: who is this girl and what has she done with her best friend?

GROTESQUE

Raine's life is far from ordinary—he's a gargoyle living in a Brooklyn church. Peering down from the church's balcony, Raine develops a crush on Sophie, a new girl in the neighborhood. But he has bigger problems. Raine's church is about to be demolished, and he has to do something before he is destroyed too.

READ MORE FROM 12-STORY LIBRARY
Every 12-Story Library book is available in many formats, including Amazon Kindle and Apple iBooks. For more information, visit your device's store or 12StoryLibrary.com.